The Way We Play

Theory of Game Design

Michael Killick

Apress®

The Way We Play: Theory of Game Design

Michael Killick
Cambridge, UK

ISBN-13 (pbk): 978-1-4842-8788-0 ISBN-13 (electronic): 978-1-4842-8789-7
https://doi.org/10.1007/978-1-4842-8789-7

Copyright © 2022 by Michael Killick

Managing Director, Apress Media LLC: Welmoed Spahr
Acquisitions Editor: Spandana Chatterjee
Development Editor: Spandana Chatterjee
Coordinating Editor: Mark Powers

Cover designed by eStudioCalamar

Cover image by Enrique Guzman Egas on Unsplash (www.unsplash.com)

Distributed to the book trade worldwide by Apress Media, LLC, 1 New York Plaza, New York, NY 10004, U.S.A. Phone 1-800-SPRINGER, fax (201) 348-4505, e-mail orders-ny@springer-sbm.com, or visit www.springeronline.com. Apress Media, LLC is a California LLC and the sole member (owner) is Springer Science + Business Media Finance Inc (SSBM Finance Inc). SSBM Finance Inc is a **Delaware** corporation.

For information on translations, please e-mail booktranslations@springernature.com; for reprint, paperback, or audio rights, please e-mail bookpermissions@springernature.com.

Apress titles may be purchased in bulk for academic, corporate, or promotional use. eBook versions and licenses are also available for most titles. For more information, reference our Print and eBook Bulk Sales web page at http://www.apress.com/bulk-sales.

Any source code or other supplementary material referenced by the author in this book is available to readers on GitHub (https://github.com/Apress). For more detailed information, please visit http://www.apress.com/source-code.

Printed on acid-free paper

This book is dedicated to my students, past and present.
You make teaching in the world of video games a little more interesting
with every year.

Table of Contents

About the Author

Michael Killick is a Game Design Teacher, Game Designer, and BAFTA Nominated Young Game Design Mentor. He is currently the lead of the Level 3 Games Development course and the student publishing company, Rizing Games, which offers students the chance to develop and release their mobile and console games to global markets. It's his job to work with upcoming game designers to show them what they need to know to create their first video games and how they can publish these to the wider gaming world. Due to his work within game development and the support he has provided to young people, he has been chosen to be a BAFTA Member to continue his support for upcoming game designers.

About the Technical Reviewer

Simon Jackson is a long-time software engineer and architect with many years of Unity game development experience. He's also an author of several Unity game development titles. He loves to create Unity projects, and he loves to lend a hand to help educate others, whether it's via a blog, vlog, user group, or major speaking event. His primary focus at the moment is with the XRTK (Mixed Reality Toolkit) project. The goal of this project is to build a cross-platform Mixed Reality framework to enable both VR and AR developers to build efficient solutions in Unity and then distribute them to as many platforms as possible.

Acknowledgments

Books don't just fall out of the sky and land onto shelves and ereaders, they take time and care from not just the author but from the supporting team and those around the author. That's why I want to take a moment and thank those that have supported me on my journey to writing this book for you, as I wouldn't have been able to help you without them helping me.

To my family and friends who were with me when my journey into games began. The Rizing Games team and all those that have been a part of it. My wonderful students, past and present, you truly have been some of the most talented people I have ever met and a privilege to teach. The supporting team at Apress, without whom none of this would have been possible. Lastly, to my wife, Beth, who has also listened to hours of book and game ideas.

Introduction

You probably have already played hundreds of games before you have picked up this book and loved, and maybe disliked, some. Or maybe, you may have never played a video game in your life, and you much prefer to play card or board games. (No matter, they will be mentioned in this book too.) But this book isn't about taking famous video games apart and pointing out their flaws, this book is about what goes on to make those games and what worked. For some of us, we have been waking up over festive celebrations, opening the biggest game of the year that all our friends have been talking about. But have you ever wondered HOW it got there? Yes, a jolly fat man might have left it for you, but have you ever wanted to know how it was made? Or have you ever shown an interest in the way a video game was made?

This book has been written for three types of people: those that want to develop their skills and knowledge further, those that are starting out in game design or students that want to know the best place to start, and those that love to play games.

For those that are already working within video games, there are plenty of books already out there that might give you a lot of theory, but they might be very formal and sometimes hard to relate to. However, this book will provide some theory but also some practical elements while also keeping things casual. I don't want this book to be talking at you, but more talking along with you.

If you are a student or just starting out in video games, I bring in a perspective of someone who has studied video games but has also been teaching it. I have been involved in countless projects and seen many mistakes made but also seen some amazing projects come to life. Over the course of the book, I will tell stories of some of my lessons but also what you need to think about as you start out in this ever-changing and expansive world we call game development. You will also get to see what comes next once you have made your video game and what options lie ahead once you reach this milestone. I didn't study video games till I was in my mid-teens, and even then, I fell into the subject! It was a strange new world I found myself in, and I quickly learned that I needed all the supporting material out there to help me on my journey. I made lots of mistakes with projects that I made, but this book will help you to avoid making those mistakes. And I hope that you find in this book some of your supporting material as you start out on your journey.

Lastly, there is someone else out there that this book is aimed toward. Those that love video games and are die-hard fans, just like me! Even if you never want to make video games but are curious about what goes on in the land of game development, then this book will give you a look into the window of this world. I have always enjoyed reading game books or game art books and felt inspired. And that is the aim of this book, to help guide those wanting to make their mark in game design.

What Will You See in This Book?

You have probably been looking around in your local bookshop or online for a book that can provide you with a background into game design and what can help you either with your career or the theory of design. You might have found some books that might have lots of theory or are fully technical. But you might be looking for one that has a perfect amount of both. So, look no further, as this is the book for you!

You may have already turned through some of the pages to see the contents list, but here is a breakdown of the things you will read and experience through upcoming pages:

- Chapter 1 – Your Design Journey Begins

  This will provide you with an insight into the history of games while looking at some of the most notable games within history and the impact they have had on current markets. You will also look into creating your first Game Design Document and the content needed. This will help prepare you for pitching your game idea to wider professionals within the industry.

- Chapter 2 – Video Games: Under the Hood

  A look into job roles within the industry and the pathway you could take. Common genres you will find within games and how these link with each other and one of the trickiest issues of them all, idea generation!

- Chapter 3 – From Paper to Screen

  As your design journey begins, you will now start to think about the important pillars within game design and how they will impact your overall idea. As movement and gameplay start to be considered here, you will also start to think about how your idea elements will start to link together.

- Chapter 4 – First-Person Character Controller in Unity

  In this chapter, you will use the game engine, Unity, to create a first-person project where you will explore the software and how this demo could be used as part of a future project.

- Chapter 5 – Rule the World – Level Design

  With your idea starting to come together, you will now explore the world of level design and the creation of the playground your player will be in. You will consider how the world will impact your gameplay and the important factors that need to be considered when creating your world.

- Chapter 6 – Friend or Foe? Enemy Design

  With characters designed, you now need to think about the enemies and obstacles that your player will face. From mercenaries to creatures, what will stand in the way of your player from achieving their goal? How does an enemy's behavior impact the gameplay experience? What does it take to create a fun boss battle?

- Chapter 7 – MCM (Mechanics, Combat, and Multiplayer)

  This chapter will walk you through three of the most important elements that make any game successful and what part they play in games we experience. From single-player action games to massive multiplayer online games, how do these influence their design?

- Chapter 8 – 2D Platformer Tutorial

  Returning to Unity once more, you will complete a tutorial that will act as a base for a future game.

- Chapter 9 – HUD and UI. What Does It Mean?

  As your game is starting to come together, we begin to explore some of the final elements and what a player will see and use within the game. In this chapter, you will explore the fundamentals of HUD and UI design and how this will play a part in the overall experience of the game.

- Chapter 10 – Parting Advice

  With your design journey coming to an end, we begin to wrap up everything we have learned and discuss how to avoid some common mistakes that are made within the design process. And more importantly, how you can better yourself during your journey.

- Chapter 11 – The End. Or Your Beginning?

  You will now think about how to create a pitch for your game and what are the best methods to take your journey further. With many ways to start sharing your work, this chapter will help guide you to what works effectively when sharing your ideas to the world.

Now as you have seen the contents of the book and hopefully you have decided to stick around to know more, then it is time to begin your game design journey. But first, I would like to leave you with some advice to consider as you read and delve into your own creative game projects. One of the most important things to remember is, no matter how big or ambitious an idea may be, show perseverance and keep going. There is no greater feeling than to know that you have overcome something and that you have achieved a goal. Always put your mind to something and never be afraid to show your creative flair and what it is you are capable of. Greatness comes from small beginnings.

CHAPTER 1

Your Design Journey Begins

The term "game" is defined as an activity that one engages in for amusement or fun. While that may be the definition of a "game," we all know what a video game is and the impact that they have on us. For those that are starting out in this world, a video game is defined as a game that is played electronically by manipulating images through an electronic device or computer. Sounds simple, but as you're about to find out, there is much more to video games than we think. Whether we play games casually, competitively, socially, or for escapism, a game has at one point in our lives meant something to us.

Before we can begin to design a game or even look as far as developing ideas, we need to ensure that we know the fundamentals of what a game is. To help with this, we will take a brief look back through the history of video games and how they have helped shape games to what we know them to be.

A Brief(ish) History

Video games didn't just happen into our lives; like all great things, they evolved into what we see and play today, but everything has to start somewhere. The 1950s saw the dawn of television, and with this, the creation of video games; however, these were played by very few people and on large computers. The first video game programmers were students in the computer labs of large universities like the Massachusetts Institute of Technology (MIT). Some of the earliest games were *OXO*, *Spacewar!*, and *Colossal Cave Adventure* that had very simple or even no graphics. These were displayed on small black and white oscilloscope screens. An oscilloscope is an instrument in which the variations in a fluctuating electrical quantity appear temporarily as a visible waveform on a display screen.

© Michael Killick 2022
M. Killick, *The Way We Play*, https://doi.org/10.1007/978-1-4842-8789-7_1

Ted Dabney and Nolan Bushnell (founders of Atari) were inspired to create their own video game after playing *Spacewar!*. Their first game was *Computer Space*, the first arcade video game in 1971. Later in the decade, arcades dedicated to video games started to appear. First arcade games could be found in bars. These early arcade games were rendered using either vector graphics or raster graphics.

Vector graphics – Images constructed from lines. This type of graphics allowed for bright, striking images seen in games such as *Battlezone*, *Tempest*, and *Star Wars*.

Raster graphics – Images constructed from a grid of dots called pixels. These spawned cartoon-inspired characters such as Pac-Man and Donkey Kong. These characters are now pop culture icons and are well known all around the world. It shows that even though designers were limited by their technology, they were still able to make something that is known by all generations, even by those that don't play video games.

During the 1980s, there were three styles of machines that gamers could use:

Uprights – Cabinets which the player stood in front of while playing (these are the ones we think of when we hear "arcade machine")

Cocktail tables – Arcade games set up into the top of a small table, allowing the player to sit down while playing

Arcade cockpit – Large game cabinets that allowed the player to lean or sit down to further enhance the gaming experience

During the mid-1980s, arcades began to appear everywhere, and video games began to take the world by storm. The revolution had begun! With this, game genres and themes became varied; this also meant that the cabinets became more vibrant and elaborate with realistic controllers. The golden age of arcades was beginning. It wasn't long before the way games were played was beginning to evolve once more. But like many good things, they all must come to an end eventually. By the time the late 1990s came, many arcade games started to resemble theme park rides with games such as horse-riding simulators and gun-wielding arcades. There were also large-scale simulators that allowed up to eight players to take part. However, these became costly to maintain and required large floor spaces. But as we head toward the end of the decade, these elaborate machines were quickly being matched by smaller home systems with much better graphics and became much cheaper to run. It wasn't long before the golden age of video game arcades was coming to an end.

Some video game arcades are still going for those that wish to feel some nostalgia of a time that once was. Some machines are still being made for some seaside arcades with games such as *Doodle Jump* and *Crossy Road*. But since the decline in arcade venues, they have become more of a social and virtual experience. These would typically appear in LAN gaming centers which combine retail and social space to allow players to play computer and console games on a per-hour basis. But other industries had begun to see how successful gaming experiences were and how they could attract their customers and make their experiences more appealing.

Theme parks and arcades were starting to adopt similar experiences and models as each other. Theme park attractions were starting to be gamified and turning into full sensory experiences. One notable experience is *The Simpsons* 4D experience at Universal Studios, Los Angeles.

Fast forward to the current generation of play, with the PlayStation 5, Xbox Series X and Nintendo Switch, which are known to the world as consoles. These are gaming platforms that can be used at home. When it comes to being under the hood, a microprocessor runs the electronic device, which sends a video display signal to the user's TV or monitor. With the advancement of playing games from your sofa, being able to hold a controller that has different triggers, buttons and analog controls opens the door to a vast variety of games that can be design and played. And unlike the dedicated motherboards in early arcade games, which could only hold one video game, console games use cartridge, CD, and DVD media to allow players to quickly change games.

Since the Xbox 360 and PlayStation 3 generation of consoles, players have been able to download video games and store these either within the built-in HDD or an attached external HDD. This allowed an expansive library of games with a fraction of the space being used to store video game boxes. This also allowed your games to be played in a range of different places and methods, partly thanks to Cloud Gaming, making games more accessible for players.

The first commercial home console like this, was the Magnavox Odyssey, which was created by gaming pioneer Ralph Baer. Technologically, this console was ahead of its time as it featured an analog controller, games on a removable ROM, and a light gun, which was the first for gaming to have an extra peripheral. Since the 1970s, home consoles exploded with a vast range of machines, all with their own technological capabilities and evolutions such as the following:

- Atari 2600

- Nintendo Entertainment System

- PlayStation (2, 3, 4, and 5)

- Xbox (360, X, S, and Series X)

- Wii and Wii U

- Nintendo Switch

- Sega Genesis

- Dreamcast

Collectively, they continue to bring games to millions of people across the world.

Like arcade games, a favorite form of gaming of mine is handheld play. Handheld games have a visual display, processor, and a controller, but are small enough to put into your pocket and pick up whenever you have a free moment. The first handheld titles were dedicated to only one game per unit, such as the Game & Watch series (Nintendo, 1980). The Microvision was one of the earliest handheld systems to have switchable cartridges. Since then, they became the norm with consoles such as the Nintendo DS range. However, the PlayStation Portable series used disks instead of cartridges.

Handheld gaming first took off when *Tetris* became a phenomenon on the Game Boy (Nintendo, 1989), which was the predecessor of the Nintendo DS. The DS featured dual screens to allow players to have a more immersive and expansive play instead of the typical single screen that most home or handheld consoles support. This then took a huge leap into the world of 3D support. This allowed the top screen to change perspective within some games and let the player view their games in 3D like in the movies. This slowly died out and was replaced with its cheaper counterpart Nintendo 2DS, which again supported two screens but removed the 3D functionality.

But games have advanced even further with the way we play them with the introduction of mobile gaming. This has allowed games to become more accessible as more of the population have access to a smartphone. With marketplaces on your phone or tablet, you can carry around an entire library of games in your pocket. Games that used to require a monitor, computer, or controller can now be played anywhere and at any time within your hands. Similarly, controllers provide new and different ways to play games, and touchscreens have enabled the creation of new control systems and genres of games.

Mobile gaming has changed not only the way we play games but also the way they are made. Games that would have required large teams and large budgets to create are now being made by small teams or individuals. Now anyone can become a game designer!

Games can now be created faster and with much less money compared to larger budget companies and console projects. However, some games are built around shorter playtimes and have become more of a pastime on mobiles. This has also impacted the way money has been generated through games. The introduction of microtransactions through games has grown exponentially. This is called monetization. This is a model where the player can purchase lives within games, customization, levels, abilities, and more. This now provides the developer and publisher more ways to earn money. This model has also been adopted by larger companies with the introduction of season passes where the player can pay a set price to unlock future game content for a specific game. This can include more levels, maps, storylines, etc. It is fair to say that mobile gaming has changed the way we make and play games forever.

With the rise of mobile gaming, it also brought with it the rise of digital distribution. Compared to its console counterparts, games could only be downloaded through a mobile marketplace or "app store." Consoles were able to support digital download, but games were more often than not bought in physical form. But with more homes being connected to the Internet, it was the perfect opportunity for games to be downloaded to consoles rather than going to your local shop to buy one. Games can now be purchased and downloaded at any time through the Internet. Some digital marketplaces are Steam, Xbox Marketplace, PlayStation Store, Nintendo eShop, and G2A. Mobile devices have iTunes and Google Play Store. Now as gamers can buy digital versions of their games, this has removed the issue with physical store space for games, but this soon required larger hard drives to store the games. As games got bigger, so did their file size! But as retailers became stuck with clients buying games digitally, physical forms soon were sold with collectable editions that include season passes, mini figures of characters, and memorabilia from the game to entice toward this purchase method.

As consoles and mobile gaming became more powerful to play games on, PCs also began to become another powerful way to play games. PCs became popular in the late 1970s, and video game programming and playing video games became more common. A new generation of game designers began by programming in their bedrooms, and these games were stored on cassette tapes that would be placed in tape drives. These soon evolved into floppy disks that were placed into floppy drives. Earlier games tried to emulate what gamers could experience in arcades, and with this, the Apple 2 took advantage of the keyboard. This allowed greater user input and birthed way we play games on PC now. Since gamers could spend more time gaming, computer games created a different gaming experience. Story-based adventure games, construction and management games, and strategy games provided longer play experiences than their arcade counterparts. With more time being invested into games, it gave players more perceived value for their money.

Technology continued to evolve. Hardware, memory, and storage evolved to CD and DVD media; computer games became more detailed and more complex. The rise of first-person shooters (FPS) was down to the popularity of the mouse and keyboard controls. The computer was the ultimate gaming platform by the mid-1990s. Even now, several gaming genres such as FPSs and massively multiplayer online games (MMOs) remain as some of the most popular genres on PC. Touchscreen games which were typically found on mobile devices are now starting to appear on more home computers and laptops, which also open more avenues to how we can play games on PC.

The Top Scorers

We can all name a game that we loved or has "flopped" since its release. I could easily say that *Pokémon Pearl* was the best game of the *Pokémon* series and that the *Uncharted* games were the best exclusives for PlayStation. While this is purely down to my opinion, it makes me question how we can determine a game that was "good." Some of that is down to a player and reviewer's opinion, and another would be down to the facts, such as sales, which now brings us to the most successful video games of all time and what has led them to their huge success. According to Screen Rant, these are the top selling video games of all time [1].

10 – *Mario Kart Wii* (2006)

With the birth of the Nintendo Wii, this brought a new age to the way we could play games from the typical couch play. A reason for the console's success was down to its motion control, allowing players to play using motion controllers and gestures that you would find within the real world. As new games were created and released, a new addition was released to what was already a hugely popular franchise, *Mario Kart*. The game exercised the use of the motion controls to play the game like a steering wheel. An accessory was released for the console that could also be used for the game by inserting the controller into a plastic steering wheel, giving the players increased control and the feeling of actually being inside the game.

9 – *Red Dead Redemption 2* (2018)

The publisher Rockstar Games has released some of the most exciting and popular games known to date, such as the *Grand Theft Auto* series and *Max Payne*. The game allows players to embark on missions and side quests in a massive open world which is all set at the end of the Wild West era. Missions would involve train chases and shootouts, giving the perfect experience for anyone that wanted to become a cowboy.

8 – *Super Mario Bros* (1985)

One of the games that started it all, *Super Mario Bros* is known as one of the most well-known video games in history. This in turn has helped spawn a whole franchise of games, TV shows, and films and has amassed billions of dollars in merchandise sales worldwide. The true number of sales will never be known as the game is now available with the Nintendo Switch online, but it's clear that the game that somewhat started it all is still going strong.

7 – *Mario Kart 8* (2014)

Following the huge success of *Mario Kart Wii*, it has become one of the most successful video games that the Nintendo Wii U ever sold. (The Wii U was a handheld and home console rolled into one, with a gamepad that could be linked to the TV to provide handheld experience. This could only take place while the main console unit was in the same room as the player which brought portability issues.) While the Wii U was widely known as unsuccessful for gamers and sales, *Mario Kart 8* kept the flame alight for consoles and continued to take players by storm.

6 – *Pokémon Red, Blue,* and *Green* (1996)

One of the most successful franchises in gaming history was born with this trio of games. What began in 1996 was the birth of a number of main series titles, spin-off games, a number of movies, and a popular anime. The total number of sales has never been known due to digital remakes being made for the 3DS in 2016. The release of these games was a crucial moment in Nintendo's history as this showed that they could produce games in an ever-changing market.

5 – *PlayerUnknown's Battlegrounds* (2017)

Despite being released in 2017, the game uses a battle royale mode where the player can work alone or in a team to defeat other players and be the last person standing. As well as the game being hugely successful for PC, the mobile version has since been released and is known to be the most downloaded mobile game of all time.

4 – *Wii Sports* (2006)

As one of the most influential games of all time, not only did it revolutionize the way we play games and what gaming could be, it helped drive the sales of the Nintendo Wii. The game was coupled with the console which also helped drive sales. Anyone who owned a Wii during the 2000s would remember boxing someone or bowling with someone in their living room.

3 – *Grand Theft Auto V and GTA V*

For a game that was released nearly ten years ago, *GTA 5* is still bringing in new players while continuing to add new content. It's the perfect combination of action, combat, open-world exploration, and story. It is the perfect balance of mechanics and gameplay and shows what the pinnacle of what a great game can be.

2 – *Minecraft* (2011)

While the concept of the game is simple, this has a rightful place to be one of the most successful video games of all time. It is so powerful; it can allow the player to create whatever they want. It plays on the imagination of millions which helps guide the gameplay. Social media and YouTube have helped amass its success and have also appeared as an educational tool for various levels in schools.

1 – *Tetris* (1984)

What was once a simple arcade-style game that was released for the PC has now amassed various spin-offs and remakes and has appeared on nearly every electronic device ever. It even became an arcade game, was hugely successful on Nintendo's handheld Game Boy, and was later released on every major console and phone, as well as iPods. Despite being decades old, it remains popular to this day and is loved by gamers young and old and shows that sometimes simplicity is key!

[1] `https://screenrant.com/best-selling-video-games-most-popular`

Writing Your Game Design Document – Introduction

When it comes to pitching an idea to your colleagues (or fellow game design enthusiasts!), one of the most crucial documents you will ever make is a Game Design Document (GDD). This contains all details and ideas about the game you want to make. This document is pivotal to giving your game's first legs and getting it off the ground. But there are four components for this document that will assist you in the preproduction of your game and in creating a great GDD:

1. The One-Sheet

2. The Ten-Page Boss

3. The Beat Chart

4. The Game Design Document

These documents all have their own purpose and help build upon the definitions of your game and all that you intend to make. All build upon each other which will eventually compose the content that will be found in your GDD.

When making your GDD, the length will be determined by the complexity of your game. If you are making a mobile game, your GDD could be 30 pages long, but if you are making a console game, this could be 300 pages long. However, designers have always struggled to pinpoint how long a document should be. In some cases, designers feel that documents should only be a few pages, but your GDD should be as whatever length it needs to be to ensure you are getting your ideas across. But the documents mentioned earlier are all steps you can take to create your GDD.

There are a few tips and tricks you can use when making your GDD. For example, you need to ensure that you are using a font that is readable. Although this may sound obvious, try to avoid using any fancy fonts. Keep it simple and legible. I have read many

GDDs, and there is nothing more difficult than to read a document that uses a fancy font to "meet the genre of the game," such as using a swirly typeface as it looks medieval and that's where the game's story will be set (its context).

There is no official format for any of the documents; this is just a tip to help you begin the formatting of yours. Just be sure to remember the key goal of your GDD, and with any great GDD, is communication. This is the communication to the player, team members, and your publishers. The clearer the communication, the easier it will be to get others excited about the game you are wanting to make.

Step 1: The One-Sheet

The One-Sheet is a simple overview of your game. This should also be no more than one page. Pretty simple? A few different people will read this, so the document needs to be interesting and informative, but it also needs to be short. This document can be created in any way you like, but it needs to include the following information:

1. Game title

2. Intended game systems

3. Target age of players

4. Intended ESRB rating (Entertainment Software Rating Board)

5. Summary of the game's story while also focusing on the gameplay

6. Clear modes of gameplay

7. USPs (unique selling points)

8. Any competitors

Sounds pretty simple still? It should be! Most of these are straightforward to complete, which is exactly what this document is designed to do, and convey the game in just one page. However, there are a few things that you will need to think about in more detail, such as the ESRB rating and the USPs of your game.

ESRB/Pan European Game Information (PEGI) Ratings

When it comes to designing and publishing your game, the content you are making will always need to be checked for its appropriateness and suitability for its intended audience. There are companies that dedicate themselves to review content that is being produced for these purposes. Depending on the region of the world you are living in, and where you intend on releasing your game to, you have ESRB which covers the Americas and Canada and PEGI that covers Europe. While most games are suitable for players of all ages, some are only suitable for older audiences or teenagers. A specific portion of the game market contains content that is only suitable for an older audience.

ESRB is a self-regulatory organization that places a rating system for content that categorizes it into appropriate age groups. ESRB uses ratings such as G, PG, PG-13, R, and X, which is similar to the way movies are rated in the United States. Games are also reviewed and assigned a letter rating according to content.

PEGI is used to rate the consideration of age suitability and not the level of difficulty, which has led to confusion in the past. A PEGI 3 game will not contain inappropriate content but can sometimes be too difficult to play for younger children, while a PEGI 18 game could be easy to play but may contain content that is inappropriate for a younger audience. PEGI uses ratings such as 3, 7, 12, 16, and 18.

Unique Selling Points (USPs)

In simple terms, what makes your game stand out from the rest? Similar to knowing your competitors, you need to ensure that you are creating something within your game that can challenge other games out there. All games claim they have a unique selling point, but when everyone can become a game designer, coming up with a USP can be quite difficult. But be careful; writing elements such as "amazing graphics" or "most anticipated sequel" won't count toward the USPs. These need to be unique and specific features of your game that make them stand out from the crowd.

Competitors – Know Your Competition!

As more people become game designers, it becomes harder to create a new and original idea. The creation of worlds and stories can be easier to make, but coming up with gameplay and an idea that hasn't already been created can be difficult. When it comes to writing your GDD, you need to consider other games that are currently on the market that could go up against yours. This ties into the market and contextual research for your game.

Before you can start to look at direct competitors, you need to ensure that you know your game inside out. When designing any game, the biggest fan of it should be YOU. But as long as you have been noting down all elements of your game within this first document, finding competitors should be relatively easy. I personally find it easy to make a main competitor the direct inspiration for my game. If I am planning on making a platformer game with lots of abilities and a simple story, I immediately think of *Super Mario*, *Fez*, and *Rayman*. Now as I know some competitors, I now need to state WHY I have chosen them. This could be down to their gameplay, story, mechanics, design, etc.

Step 2: The Ten-Page Boss

Now that you have outlined the game and what you are intending on making, you now need to write about the details that will flesh out your game.

This document will essentially be the spine of your game, and publishers and designers will be able to understand the full content of your game. While this may seem like a long document, trying to keep it interesting and engaging can be a challenge. You need to ensure that the people reading this will want to invest time and potentially money into your project. No pressure! Whatever the document you are writing, the objective is to make it interesting and to keep the reader continuing to read it.

Page 1: Title Page

The easiest of the pages to make! It should contain the following:

1. Game title

2. Intended game systems

3. Target age of players

4. Intended ESRB rating

5. Projected release date

Logos

When creating your title for your document, you can create a placeholder logo until you have decided on your final one later in development. But remember (once again!) to keep it simple. With simplicity, you can however play around with different fonts to convey the genre you are intending to create for your game.

Page 2: Game Outline

There are two main parts to this page, a summary of the game story and the game flow.

Game Story

You need to follow the One-Sheet document that you created and use that as a starting point. Just be careful that you don't turn this into a novel; this only needs to be a couple of paragraphs that summarize the game story. Make sure that you give a good chunk of the story within this; your reader needs to know what will inevitably happen in your game.

Game Flow

Again, this needs to be simple and explain the flow of the game's actions while referencing the locations that your game will be set. If your game will only be set in one place, make sure that you provide enough detail about how the game will flow within just one environment. An example would be: "*Uncharted: Drake's Fortune* is a third-person action-adventure game that follows the life of fortune hunter Nathan Drake in his quest to an uncharted island to find the lost city of Eldorado where he hopes to seek his fortune."

Keeping it brief shows the genre, the camera angle, who they are playing, a broad perspective of the location, and the ultimate goal of the game and story.

While you need to keep the game flow clear, there are a few questions that you can answer within this:

- How do progression/rewards work? How will the player grow with each level as difficulty increases?

- What is the win condition for the game? What brings the story to a close?

- How will gameplay tie into the story? Will boss fights provide progression for the player and elements to the story?

- How can the player overcome challenges? Is this shown through the storytelling?

There are some cases where games don't have a main character, such as *Candy Crush*. So, you will need to concentrate on the gameplay and environments that the player will travel to.

Page 3: Character

So far within your documents, you have given a round idea on who your character is going to be and what they'll do and how they will be controlled by the player. In this page, you start to highlight a few specifics about the character. This starts to feel like a scientific report where you mention age, sex, gender, etc. But make sure that only things that are going to be mentioned or shown within your game need to appear here, such as family backgrounds.

You also need to consider the appearance of your character. What will they look like? What will they wear? What is their backstory? What is their personality like? When designing, you need to ensure that actions of the player reflect on what their personality is.

Once you have thought about all of the above for your character, you now need to think about how this relates back to gameplay. Will your character have special abilities/weapons? What mechanics will they have?

One of the best things, I find, when filling out this page, is to complete a controller map for your character. The best way to do this is to find an image of a controller or the peripheral that you are using for your game and show where the controls are going to go. A peripheral is a device that you use to play a game, such as a controller, joystick, mouse, keyboard, etc.

Page 4: Gameplay

Now you can start to think about the genre of your game and your sequence of play. Are you intending on having chapters? Will you use levels or rounds? Will you be having a nonlinear or linear storyline? This is the best chance for you to grip your reader for what they will expect from your game. If you are intending on having some large-scale levels or action-packed elements, now is your chance to sell them. Be sure to refer back to your USPs here so you can keep them fresh in your reader's mind. Some readers like to see visuals so they can try to imagine what you are wanting to make. If you can add in any diagrams or images, this will swing in your favor.

Once you have finished talking about the gameplay, you can now start to think about how the player will benefit from using their systems hardware. Will the game be downloadable? Will it be a player using motion controls or not? Will you develop a multiplayer option? Will there be a social element to your game? By stating these details, your reader will get a better understanding of what requirements will be needed to play the game.

Page 5: Game World

For this section, you need to be able to present some images of your game world. This will help the reader get a good idea on the worlds and environments you are wanting to make. It's also worth noting any environments that will appear in the story and what the player will be doing within them. Will they be looking for anything? What sort of enemies will they find? How will the environment impact the story? Flow charts are an effective method to show how the player will navigate the world. Include as much detail as possible so the reader can imagine what you are wanting to make.

Page 6: Game Experience

This section refers to the experience that you want your player to feel. It also refers to how you are going to make the player feel they are getting a complete experience; this could refer to the camera, music, cinematics, etc. All of these elements come together to make the game feel like a complete experience.

You now need to think about how this will be portrayed for the player. What are you going to get the player to see when they first start the game? What do you want your player to feel while playing? How will the use of sound and music be used to set the mood?

Page 7: Game Mechanics

One of the best parts to complete for this document is to consider the mechanics and obstacles that the player will use and face during the game.

A mechanic is considered as something the player will interact with to create or aid gameplay. Some could be from gliding, wall running, or moving platforms.

An obstacle is a mechanic that could harm or defeat the player but is often something that tends to be static, for example, spikes, pits, buzz saws, blades, etc.

You need to consider what sort of mechanics you are wanting to feature within your game. How will your player react to them? How will they help assist with your overall gameplay experience?

Other interactable items can be power-ups and collectibles. Power-ups are used to help enhance gameplay, such as infinite ammunition, extra lives, or invincibility. Not all games use these, but they feature in more platformer and racing games. Collectibles can be collected by your player and can have an immediate impact on the gameplay. Some games use them to encourage the player to explore environments and levels to achieve 100% completion, and some use them as part of monetary experience. Your game might have a currency in which they will be able to purchase power-ups or gear/appearance modifiers. If your game will have a currency system, be sure to explain what the player will need to do to collect money and what they will be able to buy. What will your player collect? How will they affect the game? Will your game have a currency? Will the player be able to collect trophies or achievements for collecting items?

Page 8: Enemies

Artificial intelligence (AI) is used in some cases to provide the illusion of other players' immersion of the world that the player is experiencing. In our case, AI can be used to create enemies for our game. This is the section where you need to talk about any hazards that you are wanting to create in the form of enemies. What will they do? What is their purpose? Will they vary in abilities or size?

Enemies can range from sizes and versions. For example, some third-person games will have some enemies that are dressed the same but are the easiest to defeat. Then you might find some enemies that are armored and will need precision and the use of mechanics that you have learned earlier in the game to defeat them. In some cases, you might have a boss fight where the enemies are larger and will take skills to defeat; these tend to be found at the end of levels and will range in difficulty. How will your enemies impact the story? What will the player need to learn to defeat them? What will their weakness be? Enemies can be some of the most interesting elements of your game, so your reader will want to know everything when it comes to them.

Page 9: Cutscenes

Not all games have them, but games use cutscenes to help guide the player through the story visually. You need to think about how they will be presented to the player and how they will be created. Also, make it clear when the player will see them, for example, at the end of levels 1 and 3.

Page 10: Bonus Materials

For your final page, this is where you can talk about any bonus material that you can include to create "replayability." "Replayability" is a theory of something that will bring the player back to play the game time and time again. This can be from encouraging players to achieve 100% with collectibles, achievements, etc. This is where you state what will bring the player back to the game. Some games have a New Game+ feature that will allow the player to replay the game while carrying over any abilities and costumes while being played on a higher difficulty to provide a challenge. You can also mention any downloadable content for the game and add-ons that the player can buy to enhance their experience such as weapon packs, story expansions, skins, characters, in-game currency, or, in some cases, digital deluxe upgrades.

While some players enjoy the art of collecting everything in the game, some enjoy being able to collect achievements or trophies for carrying out certain tasks within the game. Using this method is a little "something extra" for those players that like to complete their game to 100%. You also need to consider if you plan on having multiplayer as an option for play. Not every game uses it, but this is where you would state how players would interact with others and what they will do.

Step 3: The GDD

As you have completed all of the other required documents so far, now you can complete the GDD for your game. Although the previous documents you have created are crucial for the design of your game, it's the GDD that your team will be referring to during development. While this is an important document to create, the information that you add will contain details about all areas of your game that you wish to make.

While this is a huge document that requires time and effort to put all the information about your game into, other designers may not read it. Designers may be interested in them but may not have the time to read them fully. But as the person who has come up with the idea for the game, it is YOU that will need to use this document to keep track of your ideas. No matter how big or small the project idea is, you can only keep track of so much, which is why the GDD is perfect for this. The more familiar you are with your ideas, the easier it will be to work with your teammates and create the game. This also helps to avoid any situation where you forget a great idea you had, as we have all experienced this at some point.

Remember that all designers will create their documents in ways that they feel are effective for them and for their game idea. But you need to ensure that you sell your game as fun and that your reader will want to back your idea. Not all designers will want to work this way, but finding your own way is best. As long as you are clear with the communication, how you deliver them is up to you. There are plenty of techniques you can follow to assist you with this.

Storyboards – Gameplay can be storyboarded to show what you are intending to make. The art style will not matter here as long as your ideas can be conveyed. So, if you are a fan of stick figures, then that will be perfect. Be sure to use any previous games or films as inspiration as well.

Diagrams – These also don't need to be perfect, so drawing out some of your gameplay in this form is also acceptable. You can draw out the elements of your game while showing what they mean and how they will impact your game.

Short animations – If you can or someone in your team, you can create some short animations to demonstrate the gameplay you are wanting to achieve. This, again, is another effective way for the reader to clearly imagine and see what could become a reality in your game. Sometimes, being able to visualize ideas is the most effective method and can remove the chance of readers imagining the wrong thing.

Beat chart – This document covers the game in its entirety. This allows the readers to understand the game fully and all information that you have within your document.

Shareability – Why not have your GDD in more than one place? Sharing your document on a file sharing site is excellent for your team to stay up to date and follow any and all plans. Be sure that it is used at the right times and that all team members are checking with it. Some ideas can always be led astray.

Your GDD will always be about gameplay. It focuses on how the player will interact with the world around them and the impact it will have. But be aware, things will always change. No idea has ever stuck with their goals and what they intend to be. Things will change over time and sometimes for the better.

Game designs will change; if you do not let your idea grow and evolve, you may miss an opportunity for you to create something truly amazing. Over time, many things within your GDD will become obsolete and may be forgotten about as you move further into production. This is where your GDD will give you that starting point to launch you into your game.

When creating your Ten-Page Boss, you need to know who your audience is. When I say audience in this case, we are talking about the audience that are going to listen and read your GDD. Game design can be broken down into four main areas (which are then broken down further into a multitude of other roles): programming, audio, art, and producer. These are the main areas and people you will be working with throughout the production of your game. Just like many other jobs in the world, all great employees must communicate. Effective communication is something all designers should be confident with and practice at. Make sure that you take the time to speak with your teammates and find out what they like about the game and if there is anything that can be done to make it better. By listening to feedback and making appropriate changes, as a result it shows great teamwork and effort on this team's project.

Progression

When a player starts a new game, there are a few different scenarios that could follow:

1. A player will follow the tutorials step by step and learn all controls at the pace the game shows them.

2. Or they will button-mash!

There have been many times where I have started up a new game, and as I move through the first level, I have pressed all of the buttons on my controller to find out what they do. In some cases, I have created carnage while pressing all of the buttons, or little will happen as some abilities may not have been unlocked yet during the tutorial. This now brings up one of the most important aspects when designing a game: gameplay progression. This isn't always an easy thing to do and may take some time in working out how this can be completed. Here are a few scenarios for you to think of:

1. The game has a level system which allows the player to gain experience to unlock special abilities they can use for their character. The player will start at level 1 with little to no skills they can use.

2. The player will be given a range of skills at the start that they would typically receive by the end of the game which are then taken away. The player will then need to progress through the game to unlock these abilities again.

3. The player plays the game as a flashback, and they see how they progress to the final form they witnessed at the start of the game.

As the creator of your game, you need to be confident with the structure of it. You will need to know how the game begins and, more importantly, how it ends. Confidence and clarity are key! This is where the beat chart now comes in handy.

The Beat Chart

This document is one of the best tools you can use to develop the content of your GDD as well as the structure of your game. This is also perfect when looking at the gameplay progression and will require the following:

- Level/world name

- Story elements

- Enemies/bosses

- New abilities

- Power-ups found in the level/world

- Collectibles and where they can be found

- Mechanics for the player and how they are introduced

- Hazards and where they can be found

- Rough time of player for levels

- Time of day the game is set

And most importantly, progression!

As you create your beat chart, you will start to see a pattern on how elements of your game are introduced and the gradual progression of your game. You can then start to look at the balancing of your game and how you can create difficulty and allow the player to feel empowered by overcoming something, such as a boss or puzzle. Although this will be on paper, you can still use this as a chance to review any holes there might be. It's better to be prepared in the blueprints so you have a solid plan moving forward. To help with this, you can do some of the following:

- Mix it up! Change the music the player listens to. If the game features the same music, it won't be long till it becomes boring. Have different versions of your music to change the tone and atmosphere of your game.

- When will the player have unlocked all abilities, extras, costumes, etc.? Give the player some time to play with them and make them feel rewarded with what they have unlocked; otherwise, there is little point having them!

- Balancing currency is key. Make sure that the player can earn enough cash to spend in the game. Also, ensure that all items can be unlocked with the total amount of money they can earn.

- When bringing in new enemies/mechanics, ensure that these are introduced in a timely manner, and so the player can use these mechanics to defeat the enemies.

- Change the world! Rather than all levels and worlds looking and feeling the same, be sure to mix it up with the time of day or weather if possible. Repetition is something to be avoided at all costs. Unless this is a main feature of your game.

If you are making a game that the player will be paying for, you want them to feel that they are getting their money's worth. By having enough content for the player to experience (and designed effectively!), then you will have nothing to worry about. There are many casual games out there and now more mobile gamers. This also brings shorter gameplay sessions that can sometimes last for an average of 15 minutes a session.

But life and games will always come in trends. Battle royale games took the markets by storm with games such as *PlayerUnknown's Battlegrounds* (*PUBG*) and *Fortnite*, which was a huge hit with younger players. But this trend may change again, and players might want to play larger-scale games or story-based games. Always try to aim for more content than less. You can always cut out any content that isn't needed when it comes to production so you can keep to the scale that you proposed during your GDD and Ten-Page Boss.

The End of Your GDD Journey

As we now reach the end of this segment, it's worth reflecting on what we have covered so far and little things we can do to ensure that we are designing and making a game that you and your players will be happy with. While all of these documents are important, they can be a challenge at times to get all of your ideas down and perfect the presentation of them. Just remember:

- Be creative! Ideas can come from anywhere, so don't be alarmed if the next big idea doesn't come to you straightaway. You have a whole team that is working with you that can help you with this. Be sure to listen to everything they have to say as they may be onto a winner!

- Always share your ideas with others. While they may not like your idea or they might criticize it, you don't always have to take their advice, but listening to them is better than not listening at all.

- Try to avoid idea changes. While you may change certain aspects of it, try to stick to the original idea you came up with. It can become easy to fall into a cycle of redoing work. Time and money may be an issue, so these are things to be aware of. Perfectionism isn't a crime, but preparation is key to ensure that you are happy before production even begins.

- Communication! As previously spoken about, talking to team members is pivotal to keeping people in the loop and checking on everyone. It can become easy for people to fall out of this loop and fall behind on news and updates. It's your job to keep everyone in check and happy with the ideas and plans.

- Show confidence in the work you do. There may be times where ideas will clash, or you will need to come up with an idea that others may not believe. Dig deep and stick with your gut. Don't be afraid to share an idea; it might just be worthwhile.

- Respect all. Everyone will have different abilities and limitations; be sure to respect everyone's. Having the right person for the job will ultimately help your game in the long run. Also having someone who has a passion for their role will make all the difference.

- Back up everything! Accidents will happen, and I have lost count as to the number of times someone has come to me explaining that they have lost their work and didn't back it up. Keep note of backups and have them saved in place you can find. Ensure that files and folders are also organized so you and others can find things.

- And finally, be prepared. If you are making a large-scale game and you are wanting to test something on level 5 and would have to play through four very long levels to get there, include little developer cheats that can help you. There will be a time where you may have to make a demo of your game to share with the public or with the press. You will also need to think about how much you would want to share in it too.

And that's it! You now know everything there is to know about writing a Game Design Document and all of the supporting papers. By following this guide, you will be able to prepare yourself and also grip your reader for that support in making the game with you. Game design will always change, but never be afraid to share your ideas!

Bonus Stage: In-Game Purchases

At some stages in this book, there will be some bonus stages that may be useful in the designing and progression of your game. For your first bonus, this section will cover in-game purchases. Although we have spoken about them briefly during the GDD, we can now go further into what they mean and why they are used.

These can take many forms, such as new content, game functionality, features, customization items, deluxe upgrades, or preorder content. These are a common feature for most games and were made popular after the boom in mobile gaming and the inclusion of this method to purchase lives, time, etc. In some cases, a player can make a payment for an in-game purchase with real money through an in-game store or a marketplace platform that is used for the platform they are using, such as Steam, PS Store, Xbox Marketplace, or Nintendo eShop. Or a player can purchase an in-game currency which can be redeemed for content during gameplay.

Some examples of this can be as follows:

- Coins, points, etc. – These can be used as the in-game currency which can be redeemed for content, costumes, items, etc.

- Levels/maps, story expansion – These will contain new areas of play and may contain items the player can use as bonus when purchasing.

- Appearance upgrades – These can be used to change the appearance of the player but are not always necessary for the story. Some games will feature costumes that may have featured in previous games released by the publishing company.

- Weapons/vehicles – Some items can be purchased that may come with special items that can be used to enhance gameplay. A weapon might come with a unique appearance that may not enhance gameplay, but the player might find it cool to look at.

Although we have looked at what they are, we can now look at why they are used. In-game purchases help enable the player to buy parts of a game that they want, which allows some freedom as to how they want to expand their game and tailor it to their gameplay experience. Publishers can also release content that the players can download after the game has been released. An example of this is *Grand Theft Auto 5*; Rockstar have been releasing free content for their players since the game's release to keep their players engaged, but they also offer the players to purchase Shark Cards which provide the player with the in-game currency that they can use to purchase weapons and items they can use to play online.

While adults are able to control what they are purchasing, it is also important for parents to understand the importance of controlling this for younger players that might use their devices to play games. While many players will enjoy games without the need to make in-game purchases, platforms and online stores will provide various tools and settings to help players make informed decisions before making a purchase. They also help control the settings relating to digital purchases, Internet access, and online interaction.

Conclusion

So far within this chapter, we have covered the following:

1. How do we start to think about designing our first game?

2. How do we write the preproduction documents?

3. What are some of the most well-known and successful games in history?

4. What to consider when designing your game

5. In-game purchases

As we now move into the next chapter, we will start to learn about some of the job roles you can find within the game industry, the range of genres you can consider, and some of the common terminology you will need to know as you move further through this book and with your pathway to becoming a game designer.

CHAPTER 2

Video Games: Under the Hood

As we have looked through the preliminary design stages for our game and its supporting documents, this chapter will give you an insight into job roles within the industry and possible career pathways that can be explored. You will also get the chance to learn about game genres and where the best place to start is when coming up with ideas and what can be done to generate them.

Introduction

From *FIFA* to *Final Fantasy*, *Mario Kart* to *Minecraft*, video games have played a huge role in many of our lives. Many of us have spent Christmas mornings unwrapping, loading up, and getting to know the next best game that year. Advancing rapidly in the past few decades, video games have gone from a niche hobby to a multibillion-pound industry of simulation, machine learning, artificial intelligence, and so much more. Far more than a pastime, video games have become a social way of life for people of all ages.

These are many roles within the industry that you could find yourself in if you wish to pursue your career within games. Most will require you to create portfolios to exhibit the skills and work you have been creating. But they will also require or look for a degree within your specialist field. This is something that is usually strongly desired, but there are plenty of university courses out there that can assist you with finding the right direction for your career path and to help you with developing your skills further. Having a degree under your belt will help support your chosen specialty, but also make you more desirable when applying for that job you have been wanting for so long! Aside from going indie and making your own games, a lot of developers are more than willing to hire a designer if they simply show that they are capable of making games. But like I said, a degree is always desired and is sometimes required depending on the role you wish to

© Michael Killick 2022
M. Killick, *The Way We Play*, https://doi.org/10.1007/978-1-4842-8789-7_2

pursue. That being said, there's no better way to learn the ins and outs of being a game designer than by going through a good program. Most schools have great courses that teach you how to use the software, give you hands-on learning, and even help you make your first game before you graduate. Also, having a game design degree (or something similar) will usually increase your chances of getting your application looked at when you shoot your CV at a game company.

It's hard to believe that after the North American video game crash of 1983, thousands of developers lost their jobs, and almost every store refused to sell anything related to games. Along came a Japanese company named Nintendo to rekindle the fire with their Nintendo Entertainment System bundled with *Super Mario Bros.* Now fast forward to today and you're looking at a powerful industry that rivals even that of Hollywood and television. This means that you don't have to worry about switching fields or learning something else any time soon. With more people playing games than ever before thanks to Facebook, social media, and smartphones, the number of gamers is only going to keep going up. All those gamers are going to need passionate designers to create awesome experiences for them.

If you enjoy the idea of creating characters, worlds, and gameplay for people to enjoy, then being lucky enough to land the role of game designers somewhere means you'll be doing what you love for a living. The good news is that the pay and benefits for designers at most studios are pretty good and even great depending on where you work, your experience, etc. Of course, most would advise against jumping into the gaming industry simply for the money. Instead, most development studios are filled with people who simply had a desire to use their own creativity toward making games for others.

Job Roles

Now as we have covered the genres that you typically find when playing or creating a game, we now need to consider the different roles that you can find within the game industry. Ever seen yourself as a game programmer or the next concept artist for your favorite company? Do you know what their role includes?

Game companies are typically made up of many members that all have their own role within it. You'll typically find indie companies have a smaller number of team members which will be in control of a different aspect within the development of a game. However, trying to create a full game on your own will prove a challenge, as this will include art, animation, UI design, programming, testing, audio, and much more.

But who are the people that make the games we play? We can now start to explore some of their roles and responsibilities within their companies.

Programmer

Within this role, using a range of languages such as C#, C++, HTML, and Python in game engines such as Unity or Unreal, a programmer will write the code that allows the player to interact with the game, creates a camera system, makes weapons work in the way they have been designed, programs physics and any artificial intelligence (AI), and so on. They have a lot to do within their role! However, rather than all programmers within a team working on the same aspect within the game, it might be that a programmer will work exclusively on creating tools that will support the team to make the game more efficient. Another programmer may write code that simulates physics within the world they are making, such as water or weather systems. Or another might be working on solely audio and sound effects within the game. Ever wondered in school if you really needed to understand algebra or wondered why maths is not important for later in life? Well, when it comes to being a programmer, you need to have an excellent understanding of maths, 2D and 3D graphics, physics, particle systems, UI, input devices (keyboards, controllers), and computer networking. Finding experts within this field is always in high demand, and some programmers can make a good living as contractors and being hired to support teams with projects. This can be from writing code and providing solutions to teams.

Artists

Once upon a time, in the early days of video game design, programmers were the ones that created the art for video games. In some ways, they still create art for games but in the forms of simple shapes. This is called the Coder's Art. These are normally placeholders until the artists and modellers provide the assets that will go into the game. Fast forward to today, you now have artists that have this responsibility.

Taking a look back through time, one of the first artists that was creating art for video games was Shigeru Miyamoto, who created *Super Mario* and *Donkey Kong*. Since then, his simple character designs are known across the world. These memorable characters were created with an 8-bit CPU using only 2-bit pixels; this means that the background elements only have four colors and that assets only have two. As technology developed, new and better hardware with more memory, color depth, and the ability to display larger graphics meant that artists could create more detailed and in-depth images, backgrounds, assets, characters, etc. This then paved the way for more photorealistic games such as *Uncharted 4: A Thief's End* and *The Last of Us Part 2*.

Just like the programming role, video game art has also become a specialist role. This means that there are now lots of subroles that come under the category "artist":

- A concept artist will use both traditional mediums and computers to create art for a game. This can be from characters, worlds, enemies, and assets within a game. However, the art is used as a reference for other artists and will never appear in the final product.

- Storyboard artists will illustrate the game's cinematics and sometimes the elements of the gameplay design which will be passed along to other artists and animators.

- We then have 3D modellers and environment artists, who use software such as Maya, Blender, MagicaVoxel, etc., who will build the environment and characters. But with creating models, we then need texture artists who paint surfaces onto objects and locations. This creates a realistic effect. VFX artists (visual effects) create stunning visual effects using a combination of 2D and 3D art.

There are also UI (user interface) designers, animators, and many more roles. You can start to get the picture now!

Designers

The role of a designer requires you to possess many skills, one of which being able to tell the difference between a good and a bad game and being able to communicate why. But more importantly, they need to love games. The role of a designer is broken down into various forms, just like artists:

- Level designers populate levels with items such as enemies and treasures. But it is their job to make the game intuitive for the player and use mechanics and skills they've picked up through the game. While a world might seem dull, level designers will make that journey from A to B fun and creative.

- System designers develop on how elements of the game will work with another. This will range from currency to skill trees. Much like a car engine, all parts need to work together to make it work; this is where system designers come into play.

- Scripters will write code for the game that will allow things to happen; this could be from an enemy attacking the player to cutscenes being triggered.

- Combat designers will work on the player's experience when the player meets enemies. This can be from working with items, weapons, abilities, and how the player can have a fair and balanced experience.

- The creative director maintains the vision of the game through the development stages. They will support all designers to ensure that the same goal and vision are met. They will also provide feedback on how they can make the game stronger.

While all designers have their part to play, they all have a key responsibility to make the game fun. If a game isn't fun, then what is the point?

Producer

This role requires you to oversee the entire game development process and team. This can also include the hiring of team members, building the teams, writing contracts, contributing to the game's design, working with the budget of the game, and organizing testing and localization of the game. You may also find that it's the producers that will be involved with any press or marketing of the game.

With producers doing so much and having so many responsibilities, you will also find associate producers that will support them. They may not do as much as the producers, some of their tasks can include supporting the team and ordering food for them if they are working late.

Tester

Quite simply, testers will play the game, but they will play the game multiple times throughout the development process to ensure that features are working, and it works as it was intended. Testers will work long hours playing certain parts of a game and push it to its limits to ensure that everything is working, but this role requires more skill than just playing games. A good tester requires patience and good communication and written skills. They will report any bugs or issues with the game to the team. Everyone has an important part to play in game design, and testers play a huge part to help us play smooth and quality-controlled games, which brings us to the next role.

Quality Assurance

Quality assurance, or QA for short, is crucial to the successful completion of a game. To ensure that we buy games that are not full of glitches and run smoothly, games are handed to the quality assurance team to spend their time working on this. This could take weeks or sometimes months to ensure that this process has been carried out fully. It's not often that a game will be released without a day 1 patch to squash any bugs on release, but updates will be published beyond the release date to squash any bugs that appear afterward. QA won't find everything, but this is where players will be able to spot some things that the QA team didn't.

Working within testing can be a gateway job into the industry if anyone would like to start from the bottom. This can open doors to working within design, artists, producers, and high-level management. Testers are just as important as artists and programmers, so don't knock them!

Composer

Something that is overlooked during game design is audio. During the early days of video games, audio used to be MIDI sounds and simple beeps and boops which would be used for action shooting. While this may have seemed simple, what was the original *Super Mario* theme made from and is that not memorable?

A composer will create the music that will help set the mood and atmosphere for a game. Music can be created on a keyboard, and they can be used to simulate other instruments. With larger budgets, some companies and composers would write music for live orchestras to make more dramatic music.

While writing music for games can adopt similar techniques as movies, it can come with some difference. For example, most game themes can be very short or will be repeated and altered to set the atmosphere.

Sound Designer

Unlike the role of a composer, a sound designer will create the sounds that will appear in the game, as well as tutorials and hints that may appear for the player on screen, but as a player, we heavily rely on sounds to immerse ourselves in the world. You could make a detailed game with lots of action, puzzles, and a heartwarming story, but without the sound, it just doesn't feel the same.

When designing a game, you can use placeholder effects until you have created the ones you are going to make. This is also a great technique to know what you want to have for your game. Some other techniques that sound designers use are blending and mixing of sounds to create something no one has heard of before and make it unique to the game. They also need to have a good understanding of the game they are involved in. This is so they know what sort of sounds they need to make but to also help the player through the game. Sounds will need to sound positive and encourage the player through the world/levels. This is a great way to show the player that they have done the right thing or that they have used a tool or item correctly.

Writer

A writer and a game designer can normally get mixed up. While we have spoken about the role of a game designer, a writer's responsibilities could vary:

- Help write the game's story to make it engaging for the player.

- Write dialogue for the characters and cutscenes. This can be a tricky task to ensure that the story makes sense in conjunction with the gameplay while still keeping the story engaging.

- Design any prompts to help the player with levels/puzzles.

- While some games don't come with them, writers will also support the writing of the game manual and any fictional support material.

- They also write the blurb on the back of the game's box to grip the players when viewing them on the shelf in a shop.

With so many new games being created, there are usually lots of work for writers. They may come and go through companies and write lots of genres, but they also need to be able to write and write in a screenplay format. Remember, writing for video games is different to writing a book, and that takes skill and lots of practice.

Product Manager

Similar to a game producer, a product manager will work with the development team and ensure that they are working within the agreed production schedule. They also assist with ensuring that the development stage goes smoothly. My role as a teacher within games can feel like this with the support of my students' games as they prepare for release. While I may set the schedule, I will keep an eye on the production of games to assist the students with their development stages.

Technical Director

Someone in this role needs to come from a programming background to help review and recommend tools and software for the team to use that can help them. There are also times where they will assess whether someone is able to make the game or not and suited to making the game they have been hired to make.

These are just a handful of roles you can find within the industry and you may find yourself in one day.

Genres

With technology growing all the time, there is a chance to reach new heights with creating new and exciting games. The bonus with this is that games are now becoming more and more accessible to everyone.

With the rise of social media and the advancement of mobile platforms, the chance to bring in new and casual players is at an all-time high. But considering all the platforms, marketplaces, and the ways we can now play games, we need to think about the different genres that are available for us to play and follow.

The term genre is used to describe a category of something; this is often used to describe books, films, TV, or music. Books can be crime, films can be action, TV can be love, and music can be rock. You can start to get the idea. Video games can also be categorized into different genres; they only have two main types of genres: story genre and game genre. Just as we described different genres with other media products, the story genre describes the type of story, such as fantasy, historical, sports, etc. Game genre is described by the type of gameplay, like how a movie can be a documentary or art a film. The game genre describes the play, not the art or the story.

Here are some that you might be familiar with or some that might be new to you:

Action – These games rely on hand/eye coordination and skill to play. There are lots of variations of games that have been made following this genre, which also makes this one of the most diverse. It is also worth noting that some of the earliest arcade games were considered as action games.

Adventure – These games normally focus on its characters, like role-playing games. They also include a range of different mechanics such as inventory management, story, etc. Depending on the style of the game, they can also include some puzzle solving to help keep the player engaged within its story.

Educational – An educational game has the primary intention to educate the player within a chosen subject. While educating the player, it is also entertaining. These games are typically aimed at a younger audience. However, there are plenty of games that have an underlying educational theme through them which help inform the player about real-world or historical events, such as *Battlefield 1* which was set during the First World War. More notably, the first level was from the perspective of a frontline soldier in the trenches and how they were rushed to certain death.

Party – A party game is specifically designed for many players, typically within the same room, to compete in a variety of different styles of gameplay. These can be from quizzes, board games, or physical movement games (*Wii Party*, *1-2-Switch*).

Puzzle – Puzzle games are based on logic, observation, and, at times, pattern completion. Sometimes, they require the player to be slow and methodical, while others can test the player's hand/eye coordination and reflexes.

Rhythm – Rhythm games allow the player to match a rhythm or beat to score points. Games such as *Beat Saber*, *Guitar Hero*, *Osu!*, and Project Diva fit within this genre.

Serious – Games that come under this genre tend to educate players while considering social issues. But games that fit within this can be incredibly diverse, as some can provide training and be used for advertising.

Shooter – Quite simply, games that focus the player on shooting projectiles at targets or at other players. This is one of the most popular genres and includes a vast number of games, such as *Battlefield*, *Call of Duty*, *Halo*, *Grand Theft Auto*, and many more.

Simulation – These can be simple games that allow the player to take their time and create their own world or manage another. These can range from managing a theme park, farm, town, or a creature. Games such as *The Sims*, *RollerCoaster Tycoon*, and

The Simpsons: Tapped Out all focus on managing an environment. However, some simulations cross over into the world of toy games. The best example of this would be Tamagotchi. Simulation games provide tools for creativity but don't always provide a win or lose state. Unless you manage to kill your Tamagotchi pet!

Vehicle simulation also comes under this genre which involves the player driving or piloting a vehicle. This can be from a Formula 1 car to a spaceship. This also has the chance to use a variety of control options such as a controller or a joystick to create a realistic or simple playstyle.

Sports – These games are based on athletic competitions, such as football, wrestling, golf, Formula 1, boxing, or ice hockey. Like action games, there are many stylistic forms with this genre ranging from simulations to fantasy versions. *Pokémon Unite* is an example where the player is using Pokémon to work in teams and get balls of energy into the opponent's hoops.

Strategy – Being able to think and use forward planning are the main traits of strategy games. This is also one of the oldest genres as this was born from the likes of Chess, Go, and Mahjong Tiles.

Traditional – While still thinking about board games, traditional games can often be based on previous physical formats. Typical card games or games that can allow the player to add bets can fall into this genre.

Special consideration – Augmented reality (AR), one of my favorite modes of games, is a blend of digital gameplay and real-world mechanics. Games such as *Pokémon Go* incorporate this mechanic to allow the player to see Pokémon within the real world. Games like these incorporate peripherals like cameras and global positioning (GPS) into its gameplay.

But this method doesn't just cater to video games, AR and VR are now being used in many different industries such as architecture, medicine, and motor vehicles. The HoloLens is Microsoft's device to bring holograms to the real world by the user wearing a headset to view models, take part in meetings, and carry out simulations of real-world scenarios such as the construction of buildings.

This is just a small list of the genres that we see in everyday life when it comes to video games. But now as we have covered these, you can now start to identify where some games combine genres or subgenres. Games such as the *Grand Theft Auto* series have a combination of action, adventure, vehicle simulation, and shooting. There are often times where minigames or activities will include traditional and sports subgenres.

But who knows, there could be many more genres created as games and technology develop over time. You never know, it might be you that does this!

Idea Generation

"You're told to generate the next big hit, the game that will take off and capture the imaginations of players all around the world. You look at your sketchbook, ready to create and... you draw a blank. Countless ideas flood to you every day but now, when it matters most, gone."

We've all suffered from this experience in the past, and if you haven't already, you probably will soon. So where can we generate ideas? What can we use to spark our imagination and begin to generate the start of our next design? Inspiration can come from absolutely anywhere and anything. There is always a game to be found within every walk of life. What that game is and how well it is executed, however, is up to you.

First of all, remember that no idea will appear fully formed and perfected in your head. Any great work has been thoroughly researched, tested, developed, improved, reviewed, and the process repeated until complete.

One of the most creative points you have during the day is just before you're about to fall asleep. That's why it's always handy to keep a notebook near your bedside. You never know if you're about to come up with the next big hit just before you sleep!

But some games have come from silly but simple ideas, for example:

- Birds are thrown from catapults at pigs.

- A bandicoot spins to break boxes and stop an evil doctor.

- A blue hedgehog with speed problems collects rings.

All of those ideas you can read, and you know exactly what they are. All of which have become hugely successful and made lots of money. With this in mind, never be too quick to bat off a game idea, even if it might sound silly.

But there are different places you can gain inspiration from to help you with coming up with ideas.

Research

Playing a variety of games, you can begin to develop a vocabulary of mechanics, dynamics, and themes that are the necessary building blocks of successful game design. It's important to stay varied in this approach and not stick to games that you are familiar with or class as your favorite. Explore yourself with many new kinds of games to develop your range of knowledge and skills. Research into how some of these games were made in order to see where their influences came from.

Networking

Discussing your ideas with people around you is an easy way to begin the process. Taking a simple premise and simply communicating your thoughts can not only help you vocalize and think through the concept, but it also allows more ideas to be added to the mix from those around you. You'll never know what someone can add to the mix if you never ask!

Experiences

Looking for game ideas in everything you do is a great way of developing your design skills. Consider your everyday life, the people you meet, activities you do, and places you go. There is a wealth of inspiration in the world around you; it's your job to make these into interesting and engaging experiences.

Reading Material

Try to read things that you might not always go to. Sometimes, coming out of your comfort zone can be the best way to find inspiration for an idea. It's not always a bad thing to have similar interests as others, such as games, comics, films, books, TV shows, etc. However, when other people get their inspiration from the same places, games will start to feel the same. Trends are also set when it comes to new ideas; some movies will follow themes from other successful movies. When some games are released, their mechanics might be used in other games. You then start to feel that games are becoming repetitive, and you may find that your game is seen as too similar to something else, and then you'll start to see comparisons drawn to yours that you may have wanted to avoid. Be sure to take time to try reading different material to broaden your horizons.

Play Games!

Similar to reading different material, be sure to play a range of games that you might not have already played. Go outside your comfort zone and try new genres. It can also be handy to play bad games, then you can identify the things that were done poorly and how you would do them differently. Chatting with friends to learn from their experiences and recommendations for bad games will also be helpful.

Follow Your Passion

While looking for new ideas, be sure to never forget your passion and why you are doing what you're doing. You never know when you'll get a chance to use something you love in game design. When you are enjoying game design, it'll never feel like a job.

While it is one thing to have a good idea for a game, will people download it? I have been involved in many student projects where they came up with the next triple A title idea with only a few months to make. Sometimes, taking a moment to think about whether it is achievable with the time, money, and resources you have is just as important. You could pour your heart into making a game that you love, but if no one buys/downloads it, will that have been a waste of your time? If a game sells, then you can make more games.

What Does the Audience Want?

You could design the next big hit and imagine it being the "Game of the Year" and win lots of awards and have many sequels, but how will you know if the audience will like it? In some cases, the players don't know what they want until it's been presented to them. For example, I have had many students come to me saying they have seen something amazing advertised at E3 and that they have already preordered it. While it may be a new game, they never knew they wanted it until they saw it.

All designers need to be born with passion toward anything they want to achieve. If they have a strong vision of what theirs will be, then they will strive for that. Gamers can feel when developers have put their heart and soul into a game. Don't be afraid to hold onto your vision, but be aware that it may not turn out exactly how you envisioned it.

While you may have this idea in your head that you are excited to make, there is no guarantee that it'll be good. While designers set out to make good games, bad games can still be made. But bad games can be the result of many reasons.

When players are playing as a character that they know or love, this gives them the chance to be something that they aren't in the real world. Games should be able to do this and provide an experience where the player might feel smart, successful, a warrior, rich, good, or evil.

As you begin developing your idea, you need to consider what audience your game is targeting. Due to the boom in mobile gaming, markets shifted to more casual games, and gamers no longer need to grind for hours to max out their players and achieve all armor or equipment. You need to decide if you are aiming your game toward the hardcore players or casual. Knowing who your audience is from the beginning will help you rule out any design decisions before your ideas develop.

Age is also one of the most important factors to consider. While games are rated by PEGI or ESRB, kids may still end up playing games that are intended for older audiences. Kids aren't always interested in playing games that are intended for their age group, they will always want to play games that are for older kids. For example, a 13-year-old may be interested in a game that is meant for 18-year-olds.

The Problem with Fun

Creating "fun" is something that can always prove tricky and daunting. There is always the worry whether you are creating something that is fun for the audience. There are always problems when it comes to designing something that is fun; it might be that a game idea, such as a boss fight, level, mechanic, etc., could sound like fun on paper, but it may not when it comes to playing it. It might work, but it may only be fun to you. Fun is also subjective; a game might be fun the first time you play it, but will it be fun after the thousandth play? This is a typical thing that happens during the production of a game. You will play it over and over and you start to lose objectivity. This is why one of the most important rules to remember when designing a game is: You have no guarantee that your game idea is going to be fun. There are times where games will follow another gameplay's style, but this could lead to it being a copy of another game. Lots of FPS games follow similar FPS games, and it's not long before markets become saturated, and developers lose their objectivity during the course of production.

Brainstorming

Brainstorming is a great way to think of ideas and how to develop upon them. But to truly brainstorm for ideas, you can use some of the following:

- Somewhere to write the ideas

- Somewhere to work (preferably somewhere quiet)

- People to work with (it's always great to work with other people to bounce ideas off of. It's also fun working with other people!)

The best part about game design and coming up with ideas is that there are no bad or stupid ideas. Being open-minded is a positive attitude to have during this process and toward others. To really explore ideas, make sure that you are speaking to people from different areas such as programming, art, writers, and audio. Bring people along that have had some experience or understand this field as this can be beneficial to the process. The more diverse the group, the more creative the ideas can be. Think about all the things that you want your game to be, then write them down.

Whenever I like to plan or come up with ideas, I like to write them down on paper or on a large whiteboard. I find it easier to branch ideas off of each other until my paper or whiteboard becomes covered in the potential ideas I could do or make. Even if they don't happen, they're always good to note down in case I want to use them another time.

Got No Idea?

What happens if no ideas come to you? What happens if you can't come up with a plan straightaway? While it can happen, it's nothing to be ashamed of, and there are some methods to help you with breaking that creative block.

Taking a Walk

I find that taking a walk always helps clear my mind. I found that when I was a student; I was walking a rather fair amount during my days off, which helped me come up with a range of concepts I could create. I started to develop some of them and some life were never finished, but walking is a great way to get blood pumping and stay active. Exercising is excellent for mental health and well-being, and it's even better for coming up with ideas.

Keep Your Mind Focused

I find that I struggle to stay focused on something if I know that something important needs to be finished first. Keep your mind and schedule clear so you can give all of your time to coming up with ideas. Take a break and deal with whatever is on your mind. Whenever it is complete, your worries will no longer be there!

Work Somewhere New

I can get distracted very easily if I'm in an environment I am too familiar with. I find that working somewhere that is quiet can be really helpful, or I might put on some music to help me focus. Sometimes, working outside is always beneficial; being able to work in the sun and hear the world around you can be quite calming.

Move to the Best Bits

Sometimes, to keep the excitement of an idea going, I find that designing and developing the best bits that I get excited about helps the flow. Sometimes, you may come up with an idea, and there are some bits that may not excite you at first as much as other parts of the game. Take some time to design a mechanic rather than the UI or audio, but be very careful when doing this. Games are designed and built around a schedule, deadlines, and budgets, so time management becomes a key part of this. The game, team, and the company could suffer from a failure to maintain this; make sure you're being responsible.

Once you have created a list of ideas, now is the time to be critical and harsh. You need to narrow down your ideas to the ones that can be achievable and possible. Remove any ideas that you don't like, and you will be left with only the good ones. It's better to have a game full of good ideas rather than ones you don't like. The best thing you can do once you have your ideas is share them with someone else. It's good to share your ideas with someone who shares a passion for game design as they can provide some of the harshest but creative criticisms if they work within this industry.

Bonus Stage: Common Game Industry Terms

For our next bonus stage, you can find some common terms in Table 2-1 that are found within the industry and that you will also find during the design and production of your game. Take a look at some of the terms to help familiarize yourself with some of the language that is used within video games.

Table 2-1. *Common Industry Terms*

AAA (triple A)	Games that are created and released typically by mid-size or major publishers; usually anything that cannot be classified as "indie."
AR/VR/MR/XR	Augmented/virtual/mixed/extended reality.
Asset	Shorthand for anything that goes into a video game – characters, objects, sound effects, maps, environments, etc.
Baking	A method of preprocessing performed on game assets and data to ensure they load and perform well in real time and do not slow down gameplay due to requiring a lot of processor or GPU capacity.
Beta	A game version that contains all major features and assets. This version of a game contains no major bugs and is on its way to code release. Beta releases are occasionally given a limited release to the public for bug reporting and critical feedback.
Build	Game development lingo for the "version" of a game. Also known as a "release" or "release candidate."
Cert	Certification. The process whereby console manufacturers test a game for compatibility with their hardware and distribution platforms. This does not include playtesting or quality assurance.
Code release	The version of a game that is ready to be sent to console manufacturers for certification.
Collision (physics)	The action of two objects coming together and touching/striking one another in-game. The simple act of your playable character standing on a floor in a house requires collision parameters on both the character's feet and the floor; otherwise, that character would simply fall through the floor.
Collision detection (physics)	A process that determines when and where an object will "collide" with another object in-game. This is typically done using an object called a hitbox that will either prevent a collision or decide what area needs to be reached to create a collision.
Event	A game action that is completed through user input. When a player presses a button on their controller and the on-screen character jumps, this is considered an event.

(continued)

Table 2-1. *(continued)*

Game Design Document (GDD)	A professional document created by game developers to fully define and justify the game they've created or plan to create, usually as part of their pitch to a publisher.
Gold master	A game that has met all publisher and platform requirements, includes all assets and features, and is considered ready for launch.
Hitbox	An invisible object created around another GameObject that determines the area where collisions with other objects will occur.
Mechanics	The essential functions, rules, and outcomes that create gameplay. Mechanics are what make a game rewarding, entertaining, and interactive.
Mesh	A collection of vertices, edges, and faces that act as the foundation of a model in a video game.
Quality assurance (QA)	Testing a game for its overall quality, which normally includes finding and eliminating bugs.
Lightmap	A prerendered lighting system that is stored for continual use in a game.
Ray tracing	A light-rendering technique that simulates the interaction of light with objects in a game in such a way that it looks ultra-realistic.
Shaders	Small programs within larger game development processes typically used to control lighting and shadow effects.
UX	User experience. Ensuring that the design and implementation of a game is pleasing and user-friendly.
Vertical slice	A proof-of-concept portion of a game, typically given to investors or publishers for a chance at receiving funding and partnerships.

Conclusion

So far within this chapter, we have covered the following:

1. What job roles can you find in the industry?

2. What genres can you create games for?

3.   Common game industry terminology

4.   Idea generation methods

With another chapter completed, we will now move toward the development of these ideas and how we can bring them to life. You will start to look at the fundamentals of game design and what you need to consider when designing a character. We will also get the chance to make a 3D character controller in Unity that can be used for a future game idea.

CHAPTER 3

From Paper to Screen

Now as we have looked into different roles, genres, idea generation, and how we can pitch our game ideas to a team, we can now begin to design our first video game and the steps we can take to start. This chapter will break apart some of the key factors you need to consider during your development and design process and tips and tricks of the trade. I have separated the design process into six different areas that you will need to consider during this process: narrative, goals, design, character, controls, and camera. All link into each other and cannot work without the other. Let us get designing!

Section 1: The Narrative

There has always been the argument within game design about the balance between gameplay and story. Some games have little or neither of both. A game could be engaging with awesome gameplay but little story, or a game could have more of a focus on story and little gameplay. The art to game design is having a good balance of both.

There are some games that have a story without even really noticing it. *Super Mario Bros* (1980) showed no story in the game except for the usual: "The princess is in another castle!". But the game came with an extensive manual in the box which provided the backstory as well as the instructions for the game. *Pac-Man* is another example of where a game can be successful but has no story, but a narrative is still being created. We may imagine that Pac-Man is running from death which is why he is being chased by ghosts (that is not true but is my theory!). We as a player are creating an infinite number of narratives for something that has not been provided. While a game may not need a story, it always seems to have one.

© Michael Killick 2022
M. Killick, *The Way We Play*, https://doi.org/10.1007/978-1-4842-8789-7_3

From games to movies, there is a typical structure to writing a story:

1. The protagonist (main character or hero) will have a desire to do something. This is what sets the story into motion.

2. Our hero then encounters something that gets in the way of their desire and causes a problem that they need to solve.

3. While trying to overcome this problem, their method may fail. But they find a way to deal with this; it then creates…

4. A larger problem! Which then leads the hero into their final task which brings the biggest risk for them.

5. The hero then resolves their final task and brings them to their desire!

This could lead to a sequel, but that is something for another day!

No matter the story you are trying to tell, there must always be a beginning, middle, and end. How you fill the in-between is up to you. Hollywood has been following this method for years, so there is nothing stopping you from following this method too. Be sure to go out and get some inspiration for this too. Read stories that you may not have read before, watch tutorials or talks online about how games have been written, view methods that others have used, and follow tutorials. There are lots of ways to learn how to write for games and places you can look to help you. How is a story told in a song? TV show? News report? Poem?

Games are interactive and require balance. As previously mentioned, a game needs to have a good amount of all aspects to make it work; have too much of one thing, then your game may not turn out as well as you hoped. When designing a game, you need to be able to know the narrative that the player will experience. Never mistake a story for gameplay and vice versa.

To help us with creating simple game ideas, we can take a children's story and turn that into a game. I am going to use "The Three Little Pigs":

1. The player will play as all three pigs. You will build a house out of straw (working with crafting and inventory).

2. The antagonist (the enemy) is the big bad wolf, who will come and blow your house down, causing you to evade and seek shelter with a fellow pig while collecting items for your next house.

3. You will craft another house out of sticks (another chance for crafting).

4. The wolf will try to destroy your house again which will cause you to flee and collect more items for another house.

5. For the final level, you will craft a new house out of bricks which will have a higher resistance rate to wind (you could add abilities, strengths, and weaknesses to each house to make it more immersive).

6. The wolf will try to defeat you one final time but to no avail. You have beaten the final boss and won the game!

Simple? You have been able to add gameplay to a famous story. While it may be a short game, you can see how to turn a simple story into something that could be playable.

While you may come across many limitations within the design of your game (but these will vary based on scenarios), the biggest limitation you will face is your imagination. No idea is too big or too small.

When developing a game and its story, you need to find the middle ground and appeal to wider audiences. This can be defined by the following:

1. Players that are in the story as it happens. Those that wish to be thrown into that world and experience something immersive.

2. Players that want to go in depth. These are the ones that wish to know the lore, backstories, and all details about the world you have created. And then you have...

3. Players that do not care for the story at all. I have met so many players that would rather skip cutscenes and just enjoy the game for what it is. (In my opinion, I could not think of anything worse than to miss something from the story which could make the gameplay confusing and lose track as to what the goal might be!)

While these are the types of players that you will need to accommodate, this can be a challenge. Here are a few tips that might help:

*   Have you thought about collectibles your player could get that give more of a backstory? This is a fantastic way to include more into the story without it getting in the way of the main storyline while also letting the player enjoy exploring the world and searching for lore.

- As mentioned before, there are those that would rather skip all cutscenes and move to playing the game. If you can reveal the story through the gameplay so the player does not miss much from the cutscenes, this will avoid any confusion or loss in the goals of your level.

- Playing games in short bursts can help keep the player involved. While keeping twists and turns within the story, it helps keep the player on their toes and engaged with what you have designed.

While producing your story may be fun and engaging for you, writing the end of a story can be a challenge. With more games becoming immersive and expansive, producing an ending not only satisfies the player, but it also brings their goals and what they set off to achieve to a close. Previously, older games used to have an end screen as the story was limited. But how long should a story/game be? Most games will average 8–15 hours of playtime, but this will vary depending on the size of the game. In games such as *Skyrim* or *Breath of the Wild*, you can complete the main story of the game within that time, but you can still leave room for the player to explore the world while also completing any side missions or quests. This also allows the player to replay the game again or aim to achieve 100%. But remember, make the player feel satisfied, and make them feel that they have got enough from their money and the time they have invested to play your game.

Some games might offer alternative endings or experiences for the player, such as minigames, unlockable content after the story, downloadable content, etc. This is another way to keep the player engaged despite completing the game. If you create a world that your player wants to be in, they will come back to it again.

Games will also take the form of a linear or nonlinear storyline. The difference between the two are as follows:

- Nonlinear – The story will take a path based on the player's decisions; hence, it is not travelling in a straight line. While the end may be the same no matter the choices you make, small details might change such as certain characters being alive for the end. *Until Dawn* is a great example of keeping characters alive through the actions of the player. There is a way of being able to keep all the characters alive by the end of the game, but the result of the player's actions will have ripple effects throughout the story. This is also a great way to give the characters a personality based on your choices. A character might not support you or talk to you differently if you fail to help them. The *Batman, Game of Thrones, The Walking Dead,* and *The Wolf Among Us* games from TellTale and the *Life Is Strange* series from Square Enix are examples of nonlinear story-based games.

- Linear – Where the story travels in one direction and all players will experience the same ending. Some games might allow choices to appear that affect gameplay, but all players will get the same experience. This is widely used in games such as first-person shooters and platformers.

Section 2: Who Are You Playing As?

Considered one of the most creative parts of video game design is the creation of the main character. I have spent many hours listening to talks from my students about their flashy protagonist and their backstory and what brought them into the world that they wish to make. Credit to some where they were able to create a simpler version of their intended character, but in most cases, they did not come to life, and this was partly due to time management. While we have spoken about the designing of your story earlier in this chapter, this section now focuses on the designing of the gameplay and how they are presented to the player.

Nathan Drake: Cocky, brutal, and intelligent

Spider-Man: Acrobatic, young, heroic

Ratchet: Whitty, lost, protective

These are just a few familiar characters within the gaming world, but these are three words that best describe their personality. Try it, think about some of your favorite characters, and try to best describe their personality in three words; it is not as easy as you think! But these traits need to be considered through the story and through the gameplay too. Also consider the appearance of your character; you can try to produce some mock designs of what your character could look like while considering your mentioned personality traits.

While thinking about your character, why not try to think about what sort of hero they might be? Would they fit into one of the following categories?

Humorous

- Will say funny things and make the player laugh. This can be one of the most difficult things to write, so it might require someone who has experience with writing funny dialogue.

- Will do funny things but not too childish. Slapstick comedy is always a winner, but try to keep it funny without it looking forced.

Heroic

- The one that saves the world, day, etc., but does it with the right morals and is good at something. For example, Nathan Drake is good at climbing and solving puzzles and good in a firefight. Also consider a specialty for your hero such as a weapon or a skill. This will help them stand out from the crowd in a market that is full of heroes and abilities!

- But what weaknesses do they have? Not everyone is perfect, but you need to think about what could halt your character. Indiana Jones is the perfect tomb raider, but he is scared of snakes. Having little considerations helps make your hero more human and real. Try to find ways to have these incorporated into your game; you will find that balancing things out like this will make your game feel more rounded.

The last one is the player we all wish we could be.

Rebel and Awesome

- Will always look awesome, no matter what they might wear, do, or say.

- Not a nice person but is never afraid to kill anyone that might get in their way to complete their mission. Your character enjoys killing others just a little more than the rest.

- While you may want to create a character that looks and feels awesome to play as while also wishing that you were them (it can happen!), you need to be careful that your character does not come across as someone who does not have a personality. Wolverine was a badass, but the more films that he was in, the more of his personality we got to see. Turns out he was just a troubled guy and looked out for his own!

Some of us may play a game and enjoy it for what it is, but there are others who see these characters as role models. There has been an ongoing debate about whether video games make players violent, or morals of the character are suitable for the audience. I found that *The Amazing Spider-Man* films with Andrew Garfield depicted Spider-Man's morals in the wrong light. Peter Parker became a vigilante to find Uncle Ben's killer, not to save the city or fight crime. In comparison with other versions of Spider-Man, this was one where the morals were slightly slanted (but this is just my opinion!). However, Spider-Man is one of the world's most popular superheroes, and this is partly due to his superpowers but also because of his morals. If your character is designed effectively, you could find that your player will look up to this character. Who knows, you may even get someone dressing up as them at a Comic Con!

Customizing Characters

Ever struggled to produce a name for a character? Well, why not save yourself the time and let the player decide! As a fan of customization, being able to choose the name of the protagonist is an effective way to feel like YOU are the character in the world. The *Pokémon* games are excellent for doing this. In every game in the main series, you are greeted with the professor who asks you for your name. In some of the recent games, you can choose hair color and facial features. But throughout the game, you are referred to as the name you provided at the start, so it really feels like you are becoming a Pokémon trainer and eventually the champion. In some games where customization is key to completing the game (*Skyrim*, *Fallout*), they will allow you to choose a name for your player and will also allow you to decide on what your character's appearance will be. You can imagine the sort of facial features that have been created! But in some cases, your name will never be referred to once you have designed the appearance; your name might appear on your save file or in other capacities. As you play through the game, you will start to become the character that you always wanted to be. You might only wear items that match, or deal the most damage or look the best, but this is one of the best ways for your player to take some of the stress off of you such as personality, name, appearance, etc. Sometimes, it helps to cheat!

Some games allow the player to choose what gender they would like to play as but remove the option to choose a name. *Far Cry 6* gives the player a choice between the role of a male or a female, but the name of the character will always be called Dani. I find this as an excellent way to be inclusive while also catering to the player's preference. Having a name that is gender neutral not only keeps the game inclusive but also stops the player from feeling like they should have picked the other gender if they have a better sounding name. A notable mention is *Assassin's Creed Valhalla* where the player can switch between genders mid-game, but both genders share the same name. Another thing that I love that Ubisoft does for their players, and to give nods to their previous titles, is allowing the player to purchase outfits or customization items. For example, you could play *Far Cry 6* while dressed as an old lady from *Watch Dogs: Legion* or Altaïr from *Assassin's Creed*. What about giving a special item or costume that can only be unlocked at the end of the game or in the final level? This gives it the specialty and lets the player think that they have worked hard for something.

More games are starting to include the option to customize or create your own character. When *Grand Theft Auto*'s online feature was turned on, the player needed to create a character that they would use while playing with friends. If some players preordered the game, they would be able to share facial features with that of John Marston, the protagonist from *Red Dead Redemption*. But players would have to consider heritage and their parents' background when designing their character. *FIFA* has also been using customization for years. Pro Clubs was a way for players to create their own player that they would be able to use in their own team while also playing across different football leagues. While *LittleBigPlanet* provides simple customization, such as costumes, you can also change the emotions of *Sackboy*. If you use the directional pad, you can make him smile, excited, sad, or at the point of tears.

Customization does not end with the player, it extends to items, weapons, base/home, etc. *Pokémon* games now give the player a chance to build caves or bases where they can train and interact with Pokémon they have caught. Liberation games such as *Far Cry* give the player the chance to expand their base with crafting items they find in the world. The base provides power-ups or modifications to the playstyle, such as vehicles and supporting teammates.

If you give the player the option for personalization, you could give the player the option to change the following:

- Name

- Appearance

- Clothing/armor/gear

- Vehicles

- Home base

- Weapons/items

However, customization should be used wisely to work with the overall experience for the player. If this is something that you would consider, you will need to think about how it will tie into the gameplay and how the player will benefit from it. I believe that customization should be something that can be seen and appreciated. If you want your player to earn armor that will provide buffs or advantages to their experience, then you want them to be able to see what they have earned to help them on their journey. There is nothing better than to wear or use something that they have earned in-game that will make their experience all the more enjoyable.

Some weapons could be unique to the character but cannot be customized. This helps keep them personal to the character and their personality and identity. What would Link be without his Master Sword or Ratchet with his trusty Wrench? It is also important to consider how these items will be used for gameplayer. In most *Ratchet & Clank* games, the wrench is used to turn cranks to move objects or unlock doors. How will your item be used to complete levels? How will they fit in with your grand design?

Most games will have a character that looks realistic or human; it is important for the characters to look well designed. If a character has not been designed correctly or does not look realistic, then this can become a problem for the player and can cause a distraction. The last thing you would want is for the player to be watching a cutscene and the character either has not rendered properly or their facial features are looking off. Here are a few things that you can consider when creating realistic and stylized looking characters.

Realistic

Facial Proportions

Something that was just mentioned was the proportions of a character's face. The only time where these can be wrong or look silly is when the player is creating their own player and they can mess with the features. Otherwise, this should be perfect!

Movement

Make sure that your player looks and feels realistic. Try not to make them do things that a human cannot do. Rigging your character's skeleton will help make your player move realistically.

Humanity

Like movement, a human should only be able to do things that only a human can do, such as drink from a glass or climb a wall and pull an enemy off the edge. You need to show a human personality through the actions of the player.

Stylized

Facial Proportions

Eyes, chins, cheeks, and other facial features are enlarged to convey an overexpressed emotion. This can be typically found in Japanese anime and games.

Movement

Using stylized movement and representations may be an easier and cost-effective method for your game. This can also help you if you lack the equipment, skill, and support you need to make your characters realistic. There are always other methods if you find yourself stuck!

Humanity

Not all games feature human characters; some notable characters such as Ratchet and Clank, Rocket, Groot (*Guardians of the Galaxy*), and Sackboy can show emotion and player investment as human characters. Again, this is down to the design and the good story writing to ensure that the player can empathize with the story they are going through.

Gameplay

You have now designed your characters; you have thought about what they are going to look like and considered their story and what has brought them to the world that you are creating. But now you need to consider the character will be impacted by gameplay. All gameplay flows from the main character, and now you need to think about their relationship with the world around them. How tall will they be? Will the enemies be taller than the character? What will be their reach if they are using a melee weapon? As you create the character, these things need to be considered. The last thing you want is to make your character too small for them to jump onto a ledge or they cannot reach an item.

Here are a few aspects of character gameplay that you need to consider:

- Height – The height of the player.

- Player's reach – This tends to be how far the player can reach when using melee attacks. This is usually the length of an arm a weapon.

- Width of passage – When creating a pathway or passage for the player to walk through, will the player fit?

- Walking speed – How fast will the player walk (this will usually be determined by how far forward you push the joystick on a controller. This will not be the case if the game is played with a keyboard).

- Running speed – How fast will the player run (this will also be determined the same way as the walking speed).

- Jump distance – This will be determined by the width of the player and how far forward they can jump.

- Jump height – This will be based on the player's height. It might be that the player can single or double jump.

- Projectile distance – Some projectiles will be destroyed after travelling a certain distance. In some cases, they will be as far as the player can see or as short as the player can reach.

Let us imagine that the player needs to climb or jump over a wall; we need to think about how the player will collide with the solid object. When programming a game, you need to think about something called collision checking. This is the method of colliding precisely with another object to avoid "clipping." Ever played a game and found yourself or an enemy moving or getting stuck in a wall? This can be down to the collision of the player and the object not checking for its point of origin.

The best place to put a point of origin would be in the center of an object. This gives enough distance between both halves of the body and creates a more realistic collision between the player and another object. You can have more than one point of origin, but this will ultimately make your code run slower. Having a collision check at the head might be useful for any hats or costume items, but you might find that your player will fall through the map and leave only their head showing through the ground. It might look funny but will ultimately leave the game unplayable. Having the point at the feet would fix the collisions with the ground, but it would mean that if the player were to jump and hit their head on something, then they would jump through the ceiling.

Moving in the Right Direction

While we are on the subject of movement and colliding with objects, being able to walk from one area to another is not gameplay. I have seen many students get confused with this meaning and use the word incorrectly when it comes to describing their games. This starts to delve into level design which is something that will be covered in a future chapter. You need to think about how the player is going to creatively move from one place to another. You could create a beautiful environment with some stunning visuals, but if the gameplay does not engage the player, then they will become bored very easily. Therefore, you need to keep gameplay interesting and more than walking!

Rather than getting your player to walk to an objective, why not get them to run, climb, and jump to it? This allows the player to practice the skills and abilities they have already learned. Lots of student games I have tested immediately have me walking through the map and make me find my way to the objective they have made. While this may seem basic and straightforward for a student game, this does not always display the "fun" and interactive element of the game. I spend more time trying to find it than experiencing it. Rather than having the play to walk to the fun, why not let them have fun all the time? The problem I find with open-world games is that there is a lot of walking to missions if there is no other means of travelling. While this might be an effective method for me to explore the map, craft, and collect items, this can quickly get tedious and sometimes boring. If you are going to make your player walk, make it quick but fill it with obstacles that can make their journey feel quicker and engaging, then they never really notice how much walking they are really doing.

Here are a few things to consider in your gameplay when thinking about speed:

- Running

- Jumping

- Flying

- Driving

- Shooting

- Fighting

- Falling

What about when you are moving slowly? Will your player do any of the following?

- Walking

- Crouching

- Sneaking

- Climbing

- Swimming

- Hoisting/scaling

If your player will be travelling via a land, sea, or air vehicle, or sometimes an animal, then you need to consider a variety of ways this will give the player an advantage over walking. If you are in a land vehicle, then you will need to apply some weight to make it feel more realistic. If a car or van is turning a corner, then weight will make it feel like you are swinging this heavy object around a tight turning. This also needs to be considered when designing a character to make them feel connected to the world. If the player jumps, how quickly will they come back down? Gravity will always play a part in your game, regardless of the world you are making. Will the player float back down if they jump on a foreign planet? Will they be wearing heavy armor that will stunt their jump height? As you can probably guess, movement, speed, and gravity are crucial items to designing a character!

Much like a box of chocolates, having a mixture of gameplay will make the game all the sweeter. Rather than keeping the speed and gameplay the same, mix it up! Keep the player engaged and provide them with a variety of gameplay elements to keep them on their toes. The world you make will impact the speed your player will move at. If your world is covered in snow, will the player be trudging through it? Will they slide on any of the ice? Much like other players, I like to sprint to my next location/level. But the sprint does not last forever. All players are given a stamina limit, but they do not always see it on the screen. This will regenerate over time or can be restored using items found in a game. Some games might have a crafting function for the player to make food or items that can restore health or stamina.

As well as stamina, some games allow the player to "dash." This is the use of giving the player a short burst of movement in a certain direction. *Call of Duty: Black Ops 3* uses this with the mech suits the player wears, allowing them to move higher into the air and carry out wall running. This also has a limit but will regenerate quicker than stamina. Dash can be useful for gameplay but is also fun when it comes to designing a level with it. You could have somewhere to wall run, but if the player runs out of dash, they could fall off. When thinking like this, you are starting to get into the mindset of a true designer! Crouching or rolling is another excellent way to help the player move quickly but evasively around the map. Rolling is typically found in open-world or third-person games where the player might be trying to dodge an enemy or an incoming object. *Pokémon Legends: Arceus* uses this mechanic to dodge incoming attacks from Pokémon in the wild and crouches when sneaking up on unsuspecting Pokémon, while games such as the recent *Tomb Raider* trilogy use crouching to move through small caves and rolling to dodge and move faster.

What kind of player are you? Go in guns blazing and hope to kill everything that sees you as an enemy? Or are you someone that likes to sneak around and take out your enemies quietly and discreetly? Whatever you are, you will find games that have stealth levels that require you to use patience and cunning to complete your mission. This is not something that is exclusive to certain game styles, such as first person or third person. *Call of Duty* has had a range of stealth-style levels, while earlier entries to the *Assassin's Creed* series began with more stealth-style levels. The purpose of stealth is for the player to move quietly and slowly. Some games may have a Detection Bar that appears above an enemy's head to indicate whether the player has been noticed. This will normally determine if your stealth efforts have been dashed or if you have been successful in not being noticed. Again, speed is something to consider when thinking about playstyle and how you want your player to move through the world.

How to Go Higher

What is a game if you do not have one of the most common gameplay elements? Jumping! Nearly all games have some form of jumping. During all my programming lessons where my students are introduced to a game engine, something that immediately follows the programming of movement is jumping. It is so basic but can be one of the most creative elements to design. How high will you have to jump to reach a ledge? Will there be jump pads you can jump on? Will your player jump/slide over the front of cars? Whenever you start to think about the player moving off the ground, you need to think about physics. Do you intend to use physics based on the real world or game physics? This is the idea of programmers tweaking the values of the real world to meet the games' needs. They need to consider the walking and running speed, jumping heights, distances, and collisions. Although these may never be exactly like the real world, having your own spin on them can make the designing of your game just a little bit more enjoyable. Now you need your physics to reflect the world you are making. If you are in space, how long will it take for your player to come back to the ground? Will you be creating a fast-paced shooter like *Doom*? Will there be a low or high level of gravity? It is the little things that need to be considered when designing your game, but they will always make the difference.

Now you need to understand the basics of jumping. Sounds silly, but there are several types you may have experienced while playing games:

- Single jump – Simple, a single jump either horizontal or vertical.

- Double jump – A second jump in succession of a single. This will follow the single jump before the player reaches the ground.

- Triple jump – Why have two jumps when you can have three?! This could be followed by a double jump onto a bounce pad.

- Automatic – A jump that happens when the player approaches something they can climb on such as a ledge.

- Wall jump – When a player reaches a wall, they can launch themselves from it. This could also follow the completion of a wall run. Games such as *Ratchet & Clank* allow the player to jump between ledges to climb up a wall or chain a jump between two walls to gain altitude.

What about ledges? What would a player do if they made it to the edge of a cliff? Would they hang? Would they try to jump off? Would they try to climb a wall? Now you need to start to think about how to climb something that might be in their path. Sometimes, jumping is not enough to get the player over an obstacle; they might need to jump and then climb. Games like *Uncharted 4* or more recent entries to the *Far Cry* series use grapples when trying to reach higher places. These ledges you try to grapple to will tend to be double if not triple the player's height, giving the sense that you are really climbing high. These ledges tend to be slightly higher than the player's jump, which will result in the player hoisting themselves over the edge. You may also want to add a "peak" mechanic to let the player peak over the edge for added stealth. Not all games need climbing to be able to hoist the player over something, but if you do decide to add them, consider the height of the player and how high you have allowed them to jump. Some games within the action/adventure genre are now seeing the inclusion of the player being able to traverse everything. *The Legend of Zelda: Breath of the Wild* and *Assassin's Creed Valhalla* now let the player climb most buildings and cliffs which avoid the need for jumping from different ledges. This opens the door to more stealth-like missions and the option to include stamina for the player and how long they can climb for. Have you thought about what your player will do if they stand at the edge of a cliff or ledge? This is a chance for you to add some character to the player with the animation or their reaction to standing at the edge. They might flail around humorously, or they might say something to remind the player that they are close to an edge.

What happens when you fall off a ledge? Or when you jump, and you want to come back down? The next thing to think about is falling. How quickly will this happen? Thinking about the player standing on the edge of something, will they jump straightaway, or will you give enough space for the player to get a run-and-jump? Some games might give the player a chance to sprint and jump. A good example would be the introductory levels to *Super Meat Boy*. They give the player a chance to learn the controls without realizing they are in a tutorial, such as sprinting and running over a large gap. Try to get the player to practice the skills and controls they have learned; the last thing you want is for the player to forget an ability that you have worked hard to design, and they never use again beyond the tutorial. As your player jumps, what will happen next? Do you want them to slide off the edge of the ledge and slide down the wall? Will they be able to jump onto another platform? What do you want to happen when they do reach the ground? Will the player lose health, or will they roll to recovery? For something so simple, there is a lot surrounding the design of it!

Just Keep Swimming!

The last movement we will cover will be swimming. Not all games have this ability, but this is always a useful method of travel or exploration technique if you ever want to implement it. Open-world games tend to use this method to allow players to either find crafting materials, travel, or explore. Some games will incorporate water into the world, but will kill the player if they try to go swimming. *Grand Theft Auto: Liberty City Stories* is an example of this where the player might walk into a body of water, and then the player will stop moving and ultimately drown. Later games in the *Grand Theft Auto* series implemented swimming and vehicles that could travel on or underwater (more about that later!).

If you want water to be a key element of your game and that your player needs to use, then why not consider making a level around it so they understand what they need to do if they encounter it? I find that open-world games will have levels surrounding new abilities that help you learn the mechanics that are being introduced to the game. If a player can explore water, are you going to have things in there to harm you? Or will it be deep enough to explore? *Grand Theft Auto 5* is an excellent example of being able to explore the depths of the sea and what will happen to you if you venture too far. If you use a submarine, you can gauge the pressure the deeper you go, but your vehicle will get crumpled by the pressure which can result in death. But the use of this vehicle will encourage players to view drowned planes, easter eggs, and treasures and avoid anything that could harm the player. But this will depend on the world you want to make. Will it be safe and calm, or will you go deadly and deep?

But how will the player use the water? You will need to consider the following when adding water into your game:

- How will the player enter/exit the water? Will there be signs to show where the body of water is, or will you have a boat or water vehicle to help indicate it?

- Can the player dive? You may want to give an indication of an oxygen meter to show how long the player can last underwater. Will the player develop a skill to stay underwater for longer? Some games do not provide that option and will only swim on the surface, but it is up to you and how you want your world to be.

- If there is anything harmful under the water, can the player defend themselves? Some games might have a harpoon that they can use or a knife; others might only let you defend yourself on land, and you need to clear the water before taking a dip.

- Can the player swim faster underwater or on the surface? Can you use the sprint button to swim faster, or will you slow down if you dive deeper?

Bringing It All Together

Now bringing all that we have learned about designing a character, we can now summarize what we have covered and what you can do to begin the making of your own.

Movement

- How high can the player jump? What are they jumping toward? Think about how big the player is and if they can reach what you want them to jump for. Are you planning on the player jumping/rolling out of the way of something? Will it be used for a defense mechanic?

- How fast/slow will the player be walking/running? How far will they need to travel in your game? Try to use a mixture of running and walking to avoid the player feeling bored and thinking your gameplay is tedious. No one likes to be bored while playing a game that should be fun!

- Will the player be able to fast-travel or move to different parts of the world? Lots of open-world games give the option to fast-travel to previously visited locations, or they encourage the player to take the long way home to visit and explore the world.

- Will the player swim? Will they be using that to collect resources, explore, or just to travel from one area to another? Think about it being deadly, calm, or not used at all!

- How does the player reach that ledge that is too high for them? How will they react? What will happen when they come off or fall from a ledge? Will they be hurt or roll to recovery?

- Finally, have a mix! A good balance of everything is always the best way to keep the player happy and engaged. You are in complete control of the design, so be sure to play and consider if this is what you set out to achieve for your character's gameplay.

- As mentioned before, will the player be climbing anything? This could be from ladders, over walls, or up cliffs.

Appearance

- Ever thought about what your player might look like if they are low on health? *The Last of Us* shows Joel and Ellie bruised and bleeding the more health they lose. In the *Ratchet & Clank* games, Ratchet looks exhausted when he is low on health, which is another way to show personality for your character.

- Apart from the appearance, how else will you show that your player is damaged or needs help? Will clothes be torn or their armor be damaged and dented?

Weapons and Items

- If a player can upgrade their weapon, rather than it just being a stat that is improved, why not make it cosmetic as well? Sometimes, a bigger gun can be awesome but can reflect its stats when shooting your enemies!

- Can items be seen on your player if they acquire them? Rather than them ending up in your inventory, what about them appearing on the player so you can keep track of the items that you have collected for a mission? Sometimes, the small touches can make the biggest difference.

Section 3: How to See the World

Now you have your character and controls, how do you see the world? This is where you now need to consider the perspective of the game and how you want your player to view the game. Choosing the right camera for your game is crucial as it does not only impact the controls for the game, but you will also need to determine how to program it to work with the ideas and world you are creating. Camera types or perspectives appear in four typical forms based on your chosen dimension.

2D Top Down

You usually find this method being used with arcade games such as *Space Invaders* or *Galaga* to show the player controlling the character from a top-down perspective. While some recent games might use this for a "retro feel," it does come with its disadvantages such as not being able to see the character or the world clearly around you. You might be able to get a bird's-eye view of any incoming enemies so you can see what's coming for you, but level design can be quite simple with this method. The popular Dead Ops Arcade in *Call of Duty: Black Ops* was a huge success by taking the zombies mode from the game and giving it a top-down multiplayer twist.

2.5D/Isometric

What comes between 2D and 3D? 2.5D of course. This perspective gives the impression that the world is a mixture of both. Classic *Pokémon* games followed this perspective while using 2D assets, and the *Animal Crossing* games used 3D assets. This also limits the camera movement in terms of it looking up, down, and in/out while on the Z axis.

Again, this camera mode comes with some advantages to using it. The player can get a snippet of what's to come in the environment such as enemies or collectibles. Enemies can also look more impressive and dangerous when approaching the player, but this can also be a disadvantage when it comes to judging whether something is closer or further away. An enemy could look close to the player when it's actually above the player. I remember playing the first *Lego Star Wars* on Game Boy which adopted this camera view, but trying to shoot enemies on a D-pad was a challenge to ensure that my blasters would aim at the enemies. But if this is something that you want for your game idea, then it's up to you!

First Person

From working with games that work with the X and Y axes, we can now throw the Z axis into the mix. This camera is used within a variety of genres such as first-person shooters (this is the most common), adventure, racing, platform, and puzzle. While this might be a popular camera form, it will come with a range of pros and cons through gameplay.

Pros

- Easier to aim weapons at targets (this is why first-person shooters are so popular as they can give a more accurate experience with shooting weapons).

- Can create a more realistic experience through the eyes of the character compared to a camera being above a character in third person.

- Items and weapons can be viewed in more detail and appreciated more.

- Augmented reality games can help create an immersive experience through the eyes of the character. *Superhot* creates the experience of smashing glass enemies with weapons found around them.

Cons

- Not always able to appreciate the world around you compared to having a camera that can rotate and view the map.

- Player might not be able to see something that the designer wants them to see (might be trickier to view the world around them and a solution to a puzzle).

As you can see, there's a good balance of pros and cons to using this camera, but it will ultimately come down to your preference and ideas. But you can add effects to the camera to give it a more realistic experience. Many first-person games allow blood splatters to appear on the screen if the player is damaged or hurt. This might also be used to determine how much health the player has. *Call of Duty* uses this method by covering the screen in blood with the more hits the player takes. If you want to use this method, make sure that you don't cover the screen too much as dying players might be at a disadvantage if they can't see! Weather conditions might be used to show the world in more detail. If the game is set in a frozen land, then the player could see ice forming on goggles they might be wearing to emphasize how cold it is. Raindrops might fall onto the screen and slowly disappear; you can be as creative as you like with it! Damaged or blurred vision is an excellent one to use to show that the player has been disoriented by an explosion or they have been hit by something. Explosions in *Call of Duty* will blur your vision but may also show blood on the screen to show that you have been hit. See, you can mix up some of the effects!

Third Person

One of my favorite camera perspectives is third person. I find that this is one of the best ways for the player to appreciate the world around them while also viewing the action and what could be coming behind you.

There are different pros and cons for using this method, one being that you can view the character in its entirety which is another way to appreciate your character design which you can't always see when in first person (unless you walk past a mirror while in first person!). You may spend most of your time viewing the back of your player during third person unless you allow the character to run toward the camera. But what happens if your camera passes through your player if you run toward yourself? Or passes through a wall or object? This is known as sorting. You can apply a detection radius to stop the camera from doing this. As a result, your camera will look like it's running along the wall to avoid going through it. This can also apply if you move your camera to look up as high as you can see, by making it hit the ground and stopping it from going through the floor.

The biggest debate that I have had with my students over the years has been the inversion of controls for the camera. I typically use the method of pushing down on the analog to look up, while my students use push up to look up. This is the typical "simulator vs. player-relative controls." Many first-person games use these controls as the default, but I always find I invert the controls to meet my needs. Always give this as an option for your player; otherwise, I won't be playing your game!

The last thing to consider is the position of the camera. While this may sound simple, think back to all third-person games you have played and where the camera position has been. Not all of them have been the same! *Uncharted* and *Tomb Raider* games have the camera quite high due to the design of the environments so the player can see what they need to jump or climb onto. *Grand Theft Auto* tends to have the camera quite low so the player can interact with the world and vehicles easily. See, not all of them are the same! This will all depend on the game you are making and down to what feels right with the game. If you need to have it higher so you can see the world, or have it lower and move more freely, then this is up to you!

Bonus Stage: Easter Eggs

One of the most popular things that my students love to implement is easter eggs. For those that are not familiar with this term, they are defined as references to famous pop culture icons. These can range from referencing previous games that a company has made or bizarre references from TV shows, games, or real-world events. The list is endless of the easter eggs that have appeared in games and what they have referenced to, but we will discuss a few in this bonus stage.

The *Grand Theft Auto* series is a perfect example of different games or pop culture references being made through their main story or in the world. There are numerous references to *Back to the Future*, previous game projects from Rockstar, Apple, Hollywood, Thelma and Louise, Bigfoot, ghosts, Playboy Mansion, Halloween, Aliens, and so many more. The TARDIS and other *Doctor Who* references have been made in numerous games through the years. The TARDIS has been found in various games through time, such as *Assassin's Creed: Origins* if the player dives deep enough in certain body of water, the original *Fallout* game, and *Lego Dimensions*. The last notable series of games that is famous for its easter eggs is the *Batman: Arkham* series and their references to famous *Batman* comics and lore. There was one example where the developers had left an easter egg for the player to find that was a reference to the next *Batman* project in the series, which was never found. The developers had to reveal the location of a hidden room which featured their hidden easter egg. You will also find references to other characters from the DC Universe through the form of audio files, conversations you can overhear with enemies, or collectibles. You can be clever when it comes to putting them in your game, but try to make some a challenge for the player to find and encourage them to explore.

But the typical thing I have seen through hundreds of game design lessons is that students will get so excited about making a game that they start to design their game around an easter egg that they have always wanted to make. I rarely turn down ideas in my lessons to allow students to explore their creativity, but easter eggs are something that I always encourage to be done at the end of production. I love finding references in games as much as the next player, but unless they are important for the development of the story or the game, these should be at the very end of your design stages. Easter eggs should be a fun time-filler for players that want to explore the world and experience the joy and fulfillment in finding them.

I believe that easter eggs can always be appreciated if implemented correctly and the player has time to find them. But they should always be easy to understand. One group I was working with was pitching a game idea to me, and they mentioned that they wanted to reference a famous YouTuber that they love to watch. While this may be satisfying for them to see the reference, the chance of other people understanding the reference is very unlikely.

If you ever want to make an easter egg, do not be deterred from making one, but just be sure that you are clever in the way you make them and give the player time to explore and stumble across them. It can be a satisfying and enjoyable experience to find them. Some players would rather watch videos or read about easter eggs in video games rather than finding them for themselves. While I tend to read about them, there is nothing more satisfying than to know that I have been able to beat a certain level that shows me an exclusive cutscene or unlock an item that I have worked hard for. It's never quite the same watching an easter egg being found in a video compared to finding it myself!

Conclusion

So far within this chapter, we have covered the following:

1.   How to design your character

2.   How to control your character

3.   How to see the world around you

4.   Designing the narrative for your game

With Chapter 3 now completed, we will now follow a tutorial on how to create a first-person camera in Unity and how this can be used as the basis for a future project. You will have the chance to develop new skills or develop upon previous experience within the software.

CHAPTER 4

First-Person Character Controller in Unity

For this chapter, you will now be shown how you can create a first-person controller within Unity which can be used as the foundation for a future project or your first game.

Set Up

Before we can begin to create our project, we will need to install Unity and create a blank project. You will need to download Unity Hub which is the home for all updates, your projects, and installations of Unity. You can find this download from the Unity website.

Once downloaded and installed, you will need to create a free Unity account to start making projects. This will also allow you to sync any projects if you log in to a different machine in the future. It will also provide you with a free license to create games on your machine. If you ever create any games commercially, then you will need a professional license, which you can purchase through Unity. Once set up, you will need to click the Install Editor button and select the version of Unity you would like to use. You can see this in Figure 4-1. I would recommend using the version that is recommended by Unity as this will be the most stable and up-to-date version at the time.

© Michael Killick 2022
M. Killick, *The Way We Play*, https://doi.org/10.1007/978-1-4842-8789-7_4

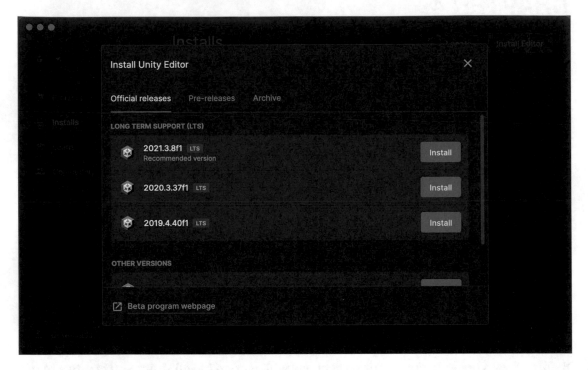

Figure 4-1. *Unity Hub and Unity software versions*

2021.3.8f is my recommended version to use, but do ensure that you select which one has been recommended by Unity to use for this tutorial. Once chosen, you will need to select some modules which will support Unity. As I am running a Mac, in the tutorial, you can see that it has been selected for me to have Visual Studio installed as well. This might not appear for you if you have already got Visual Studio installed on your machine. If you decide to use another code editor, then you can untick Visual Studio to be added. You will need to scroll through the list and choose either Mac Build Support or Windows Build Support, depending on the machine you are using. You are now ready to begin the install!

Once the software has been installed, you can now create a new project. Click the blue button which says New Project. On the left-hand side, choose Core. Then select 3D and give the project a name, such as "FSP Test Build." You can see this in Figure 4-2. When you are ready, click Create Project and wait for Unity to open!

Figure 4-2. *Unity Hub with the selection of templates*

Step 1

Create an Empty Object as shown in Figure 4-3 and then name this "First Person Player."
Then put this somewhere in the center of the scene.

Figure 4-3. *Unity Hierarchy and creation of assets*

Step 2

Under the First Person Player object, click the Add Component button under the Inspector. Then choose the character controller. Click Gizmos at the top right of the scene so you can then see the character controller in the scene, as depicted in Figure 4-4.

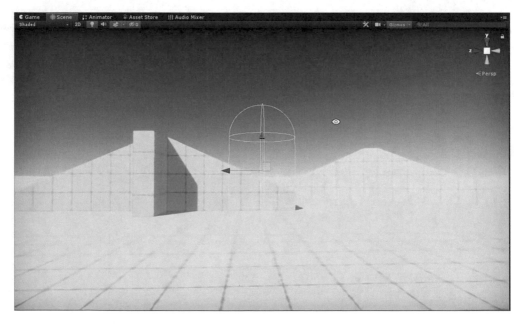

Figure 4-4. *Scene view with character controller*

Step 3

Set the values of the character controller to the following. This will allow the player to take the form of a normal size human. This can be seen in Figure 4-5.

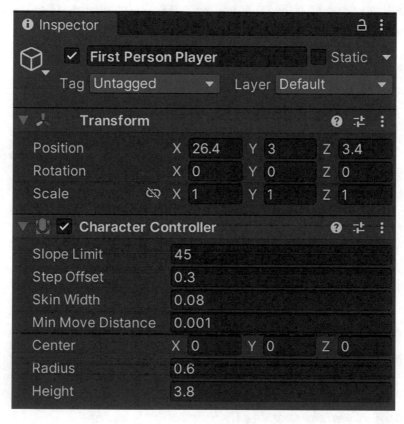

Figure 4-5. *First Person Player in the Inspector*

Radius = 0.6

Height = 3.8

Step 4

We now want to add some graphics to the player to make it feel more realistic. Go ahead and right-click the First Person Player object in the Hierarchy and add a 3D Object – Cylinder. This will generate an object that will act as your player, which has been depicted in Figure 4-6.

Figure 4-6. *Unity Hierarchy showing Cylinder object creation*

Step 5

Be sure to then set the Scale to the following so this matches the same size as your First Person Player object. You also need to remove the Capsule Collider as we will be making our own collisions later in the lesson. You can do so by clicking the cog on the far right of the component or by right-clicking the Capsule Collider component and clicking "Remove Component." You can see this in Figure 4-7.

Scale:

X = 1.2

Y = 1.8

Z = 1.2

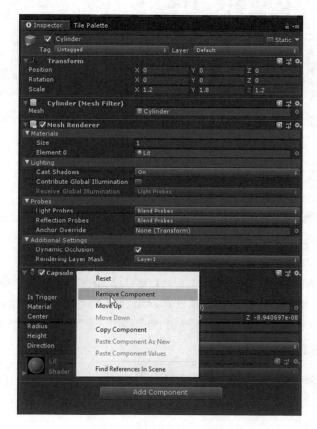

Figure 4-7. *Cylinder in the Inspector and removing the Capsule Collider component*

Step 6

The next step is to attach a camera to the player so we can see the game from a first-person perspective. Drag the main camera in the scene onto your Player object. You then need to reset the transform position from the Transform option on the Inspector. You also need to drag the camera in the scene to where the head would be on your player, so the camera is eye level. Have a look at Figure 4-8.

Figure 4-8. *Dragging the camera to make it a child of the First Person Player*

Step 7

We now need to set up the script which will allow the player to look around. This will work using the X and Y axes and will be locked so they can only look around a certain amount. This is called clamping.

Under the Inspector of your camera, click Add Component and start to type MouseLook. This will create a new C# script with that name. Once created, double-click the script which will then open your default code editor. When ready, you will need to add in the following programming:

```
public class MouseLook : MonoBehaviour
{

    public float mouseSensitivity = 100f;

    public Transform playerBody;

    float xRotation = 0f;

    void Start()
    {x
        Cursor.lockState = CursorLockMode.Locked;
    }
```

```
void Update ()
{
    float mouseX = Input.GetAxis("Mouse X") * mouseSensitivity
    * Time.deltaTime;
    float mouseY = Input.GetAxis("Mouse Y") * mouseSensitivity
    * Time.deltaTime;

    xRotation -= mouseY;
    xRotation = Mathf.Clamp(xRotation, -90f, 90f);

    transform.localRotation = Quaternion.Euler(xRotation, 0f, 0f);
    playerBody.Rotate(Vector3.up * mouseX);
}

}
```

When writing the script, it is handy to know a few things about it. We have begun by setting up some variables which will hold values for our camera, such as mouseSensitivity, which will allow you to change how sensitive the mouse will be when aiming. During our Start Event (void Start), we are locking the cursor, which means that this will not appear in the game while testing/playing. (When running the game and you wish for your cursor to reappear, press Escape on your keyboard.) mouseX and mouseY are both inputs that are built into Unity's library, which have already been given a button or a gesture. These have been set up to work with the mouse if it were to move up or down, which, in turn, will allow the player to look up and down. And Mathf. Clamp(xRotation, -90f, 90f) is locking how far the player can look up and down. No person can roll their head backward to see behind them, so why should your character do that too?

If completed correctly, you should now have a working script that allows the player to look around the world. Make sure that you test this just to be sure that everything has worked!

Step 8

Now go to your Player object and create a new script called PlayerMovement. The difference is with this script, we no longer need a void Start Event. Be sure to delete this so the void Update remains. When ready, open this script in your code editor and add in the following programming into the new script:

```
public class PlayerMovement : MonoBehaviour
{
    public CharacterController controller;

    public float speed = 12f;
    public float gravity = -9.81f;

    Vector3 velocity;

    void Update()
    {
        float x = Input.GetAxis("Horizontal");
        float z = Input.GetAxis("Vertical");

        Vector3 move = transform.right * x + transform.forward * z;

        controller.Move(move * speed * Time.deltaTime);

        velocity.y += gravity * Time.deltaTime;

        controller.Move(velocity * Time.deltaTime;
    }
}
```

Just as before, here is a little recap of some of the things we have written about in the script. The CharacterController refers to the component we attached to the Player object at the start of this tutorial and will interact with our code to create movement for our character. The public floats for speed and gravity are default values which can be changed later depending on your game idea. With these variables being made "public," it allows you to edit these values within the Inspector without the need of opening the movement script if you need to make any changes or adjustments.

Floats X and Z refer to moving the player forward and the direction the player is looking. Just like Mouse X and Mouse Y, these functions are built into Unity's library and are binded to the arrow keys and WASD. And our Vector3 move = transform.right * x + transform.forward * z refers to our functions multiplying by each other to create movement. Imagine only one of the character's legs working, neither can work without the other!

If completed correctly, you should now have a working movement script. However, in order for us to test our movement script, we will need a surface that our character can move across. Refer to Figure 4-9. To create a simple ground object, right-click in the Hierarchy and move down to 3D Object and choose Plane. Name this Environment. This will create a 2D surface that your player will be able to move around on. Make sure that you align this surface with the base of your character so it is standing on it.

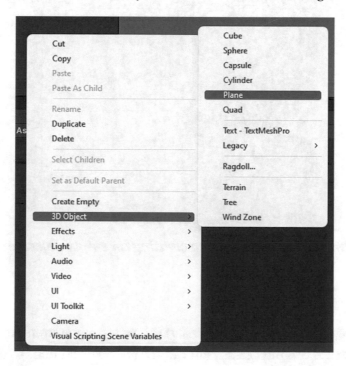

Figure 4-9. *Creating a Plane from the Hierarchy*

Step 9

We now want to make a Ground Check object which will allow the player to interact with the ground if the player jumps. This will act as precise collision checking and ensure that your player is interacting with the ground beneath them. There are different methods to create this and to avoid this situation from happening, but this is a simple method that is not just used in Unity for 3D games but can also be used when creating 2D games. Right-click the player in the Hierarchy and create an Empty Game Object. This object then needs to be dragged to the bottom of the Player object in the scene. You also need to rename this to Ground Check under the Inspector. You can see this in Figure 4-10.

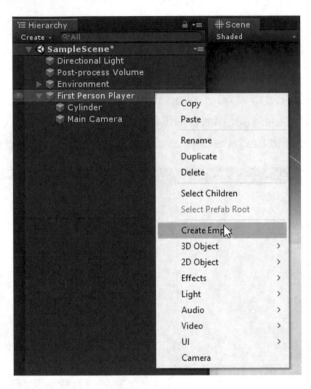

Figure 4-10. *Unity Hierarchy showing creating an empty object for Ground Check*

Step 10

Now return to the movement script and insert this new programming so collisions can now be applied to the Ground Check. You can see the new additions to the script which are highlighted in bold:

```
public class PlayerMovement : MonoBehaviour
{
    public CharacterController controller;

    public float speed = 12f;
```

```
public float gravity = -9.81f;

public Transform groundCheck;
public float groundDistance = 0.4;
public LayerMask groundMask;

Vector3 velocity;
bool isGrounded;

void Update()
{
    isGrounded = Physics.CheckSphere(groundCheck.position,
    groundDistance, groundMask);

    if(isGrounded && velocity.y < 0)
    {
        velocity.y = -2fp;
    }

    float x = Input.GetAxis("Horizontal");
    float z = Input.GetAxis("Vertical");

    Vector3 move = transform.right * x + transform.forward * z;

    controller.Move(move * speed * Time.deltaTime);

    velocity.y += gravity * Time.deltaTime;

    controller.Move(velocity * Time.deltaTime;
    }
}
```

To complete this step, click and drag the Ground Check object from the Hierarchy to the Inspector under the Ground Check float. Refer to Figure 4-11.

Figure 4-11.   *First Person Player in the Inspector and applying the Ground Check object*

Step 11

We now need to set up the layer for the ground that the player will be able to interact with when jumping. To create a new layer, go to the layer option on the right-hand side and choose Add Layer. Refer to Figure 4-12.

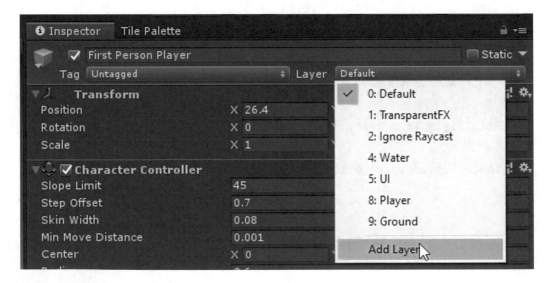

Figure 4-12.   *First Person Player in the Inspector to change the Layer type*

Then create a new layer called Ground in a black Builtin Layer box. You can see this in Figure 4-13.

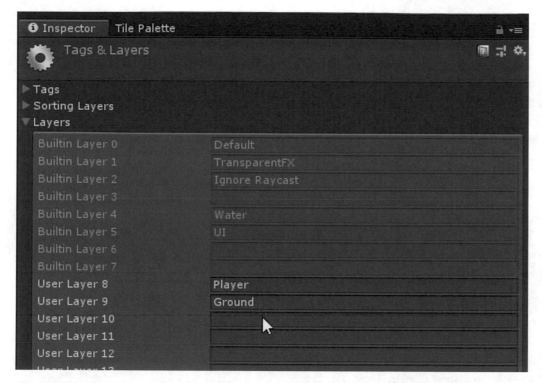

Figure 4-13. *Layer settings in the Inspector to create a new Ground layer*

Return to the Player object, and then in the Inspector, under the option of Ground Mask, choose the new Ground layer you created. This is shown in Figure 4-14.

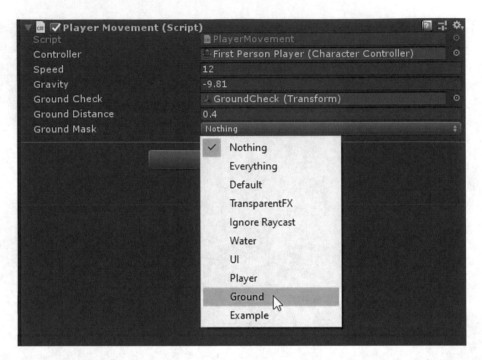

Figure 4-14. *First Person Player Inspector and applying the Ground layer to the PlayerMovement script*

To be sure that your environment is interactable, you will need to click your environment object or the object that your player walks upon and change the layer to Ground. Take a look at Figure 4-15.

Figure 4-15. *Environment in the Inspector and applying the Ground layer*

Step 12

To complete this tutorial, we will now add the ability to jump into our game. To do this, return to your PlayerMovement script again and add in the following code which has been highlighted in **bold**:

```
public class PlayerMovement : MonoBehaviour
{
    public CharacterController controller;

    public float speed = 12f;
    public float gravity = -9.81f;
    public float jumpHeight = 3f;

    public Transform groundCheck;
    public float groundDistance = 0.4;
    public LayerMask groundMask;

    Vector3 velocity;
    bool isGrounded;

    void Update()
```

```
    {
        isGrounded = Physics.CheckSphere(groundCheck.position,
        groundDistance, groundMask);

        if(isGrounded && velocity.y < 0)
        {
            velocity.y = -2fp;
        }

        float x = Input.GetAxis("Horizontal");
        float z = Input.GetAxis("Vertical");

        Vector3 move = transform.right * x + transform.forward * z;

        controller.Move(move * speed * Time.deltaTime);

        if(Input.GetButtonDown("Jump") && isGrounded)
        {
            velocity.y = Mathf.Sqrt(jumpHeight * -2f * gravity);
        }

        velocity.y += gravity * Time.deltaTime;

        controller.Move(velocity * Time.deltaTime;
    }
}
```

You can now run your game! This should mean that you now have a fully working first-person controller which can be the start of a new FPS game!

Bonus Stage: Common Unity Terms

As a bonus, Table 4-1 lists some common Unity terms that are used when working within the engine. If you decide to develop your skills further within this engine, these terms will be useful!

Table 4-1. *Common Unity Terms*

Asset Store	A Unity website that lets you download premade assets for use in your game development projects. Unity developers can also publish their own premade assets to the Asset Store for other developers to download and use.
Bool	A Boolean is a variable which can go two ways, on or off. This can be used to define is a situation is seen as True or False.
Camera	***Orthographic camera*** A camera view that makes objects appear fixed on the screen, regardless of their actual distance from one another or their relative positions. This is commonly used for retro-style 2D games, as it can make GameObjects look flat, or 2.5D games (2D games that utilize 3D elements), specifically because they allow for touches of 3D depth and definition while maintaining an otherwise 2D appearance. ***Perspective camera*** A camera view that projects objects according to their actual placement and distance on screen, giving viewers a sense of their real-world positions. This is commonly used for fully 3D titles.
Component	Something that is attached to a GameObject to alter its functionality.
Editor	The dashboard on which all of Unity's functionality is made available to its users.
Entity	A GameObject that receives components for functionality.
Public float	A variable that contains a numeric value stored in a floating point. This can be changed within the Inspector of Unity.
Private float	A variable that contains a numeric value stored in a floating point. This can only be changed within the script it was created in.
GameObject	Characters, props, and scenery in Unity.
Hierarchy window	A window in the Unity Editor that displays all GameObjects currently being used in your Scene.
Inspector window	The window in which you can view and edit the properties and settings of almost everything that appears in the Unity Editor, including assets, GameObjects, and the Editor itself.

(continued)

Table 4-1. (*continued*)

Instance	A specific version of a GameObject created from a template and modified to carry specific traits and behaviors that differentiate it from its original form.
Instantiation	The creation of an instance.
Materials	Editor objects that store the properties of surfaces in Unity, such as texture, shader, and color tint settings.
Package	A container that holds any combination of Assets, Shaders, Textures, plug-ins, icons, and scripts that enhance various parts of your project.
Package Manager	A feature within the Unity Editor that allows you to download and install add-ons and enhancements (packages) for the Unity Editor.
Prefab	A typically customized, reusable version of a GameObject.
ProBuilder	A Unity feature that enables designers to build, edit, and texture custom 3D geometry for in-scene level design.
Project window	Effectively the file finder in Unity. This is where you will be able to dive into your Scene, Asset, Prefab, and other folders.
Rigidbody	A component in Unity that lends a GameObject the ability to react to its environment through physics, for instance, giving a GameObject mass.
Runtime	The rendered, platform-specific output (e.g., for iOS, Android, Oculus, or PlayStation 4) from a Unity project.
Scene	The entire editable area in which a game can be built. Environments, props, obstacles, NPCs, menu functions, and more can be a part of each Scene in Unity.
Shader Graph	A visual Shader editing tool in Unity that lets developers create Shaders without having to write code.
Timeline	A feature in Unity for creating cinematic content, gameplay sequences, audio sequences, and complex particle effects.
Time. DeltaTime	This property provides the time between the current and the previous frame.
UI Elements	A unified UI editing tool in Unity. As of Unity 2020.1, this is known as the UI Toolkit.
Vector3	Creates a new vector with given x, y, z components.
Visual Effect Graph	A node-based visual effect editor that lets developers author visual effects that Unity simulates directly on the GPU.

Conclusion

So far within this chapter, we have covered the following:

1. How to use Unity

2. How do you program your character?

3. Setting up a camera to view your world

With Chapter 4 now completed, we will now begin to look at the designing of your world and a favorite topic of mine, level design. This will look into the fundamentals of "fun" and how to be creative with the levels you intend to make. To help prepare yourself for this chapter, start to think about some games you have played and thought they either had excellent looking graphics or were cleverly designed to suit the story and the gameplay. We will be thinking about a lot of games during this next chapter!

CHAPTER 5

Rule the World – Level Design

We have looked at the designing of a character and the movement of a camera, and now you are ready to design the world for your game. From far-flung reaches of space to blistering snowy wastelands, this is where you now get to bring your ideas to life. But where do you start? How can you make your world fun? Will your player enjoy what you have made? What will be in your world? These are all things that you need to consider during this chapter while also thinking about how you can move the character around your world. Let us now investigate one of my favorite areas of game design.

Your World

Just like other terminology within this book and in games, the word level can come with different meanings, from describing the height of something, rounds, environments, or progression. But the funny thing is, a level is not always given that name, it can be referred to by different forms of play and design. Look at some of them:

- Rounds – This is where the gameplay tends to be the same but might increase in difficulty. *Call of Duty: Zombies* is a perfect example for the use of rounds as the more enemies spawn, the higher the round. You might be able to accumulate points through this method and test the player's skill.

- Waves – These appear as combat but will have an end to them. You might find that your character ventures into uncharted territory and faces off against waves of enemies. Once they have been defeated, then your character can progress to the next stage or area.

© Michael Killick 2022
M. Killick, *The Way We Play*, https://doi.org/10.1007/978-1-4842-8789-7_5

- World – This is the game space in its entirety. This will be the setting for the game and be as expansive and vast as you like. There can be various locations for the player to explore but will be filled with missions, enemies, collectibles, side quests, etc. While your world might have various locations, it will need to follow the same theme. *Grand Theft Auto V* is made up of desert and cityscapes, but all follow the same theme of being violent, and areas are accessible for the player, such as gun shops, clothing shops, and safehouses. In early days of video games, worlds meant something completely different. Worlds would be groups of levels that might have a different theme, such as Ice World, Fire World, or Earth World. Each comes with their own levels and enemies that make them unique.

- Acts/chapters – These tend to be used if the designer wants to focus the game around the storytelling. *Life Is Strange* uses this method to show the development of the story and make it feel like the player is part of the storytelling.

These are the most common forms of levels that you will have experienced during your time of playing games. But now we need to think about the game's setting and where you would like your game to be set. It can be difficult to make a game world set somewhere new and unique. So many games have been set in a dystopian/post-apocalyptic future that it now feels that the market has become saturated. This leaves a lot of pressure on the designers to pitch a unique and fresh take on this. *The Last of Us* did it perfectly through their powerful storytelling and gameplay. But what about being set in space? I can already think of *No Man's Sky*, *Halo*, any *Star Wars* game, and *Alien*. The list goes on! But what other settings are there? Here are a few that we can look at:

- Space – Being away from Earth, it gives you more freedom to think about what life might be like beyond the stars. You can explore vast planets, experience innovative technology, use new weapons, construct ships, and take your chances in space warfare. *Halo: Combat Evolved* paved the way for a plethora of first-person shooters set in space as this was the first of its kind to use modern technology to create a fast-paced, story-driven game. Since then, we have seen *Doom* remakes, *Call of Duty* being set in space, more *Halo* games, *Destiny*, *Dead Space*, and so many more. The perfect genre for all geeks and nerds!

- Jungle – Most popular among the tomb raider and fortune hunter fans. The perfect setting for those that wish to seek long forgotten treasures and complete puzzles to take them into tombs and avoid traps. This is a fantastic way to introduce creatures that can typically be found in this environment such as crocodiles and snakes. This area is less likely to have vehicles that the player can use but gives the chance to go off the beaten track and explore on foot. Or the player might swing from vines, swim, or climb, a great chance to explore different mechanics within this setting.

- Hospital/haunted house – For all those horror fans and that like jump scares, this is the setting for you. Players will explore creepy environments and not know what they might face up ahead. Giving the fear of the unknown is the best way to instill fear into the player. Music and lighting are crucial to this to ensure that the mood is being set along with a strong story. Be sure to create moments of silence or quiet, so when something jumps out at the player, it will create the perfect scare! *Outlast* is perfect for this by giving the player the goal to collect evidence that the asylum is not fit for purpose and then giving the player the goal to escape. With the use of humans and creatures jumping out and screaming at the player, this is perfect to fill your environment with those elements to make the world feel scary.

- Pirate – Ever seen yourself as a swashbuckler and to sail the Seven Seas? Then this is the setting for you! Filled with weapons, treasure, and explosions, this is a great setting for exploration and the chance to visit islands and plunder treasure. This is a great setting for action and sailing your ship to destroy enemies that wish to steal your treasure. Then you have the shanties. You can never forget about having your crew sing shanties as you cross the seas. This is a perfect method if this is something you are wanting to explore for your game.

- Cityscape/urban – When you think of games set in cities, what do you think of? I may have mentioned the *Grand Theft Auto* series a few times so far in this book, but they fit perfectly here. This style is perfect if you are wanting gangs, customizable vehicles, heists, and a wide variety of weapons. This is also one of the most realistic settings you can go for to make it feel that the player is part of that world. An easier setting to design, buildings and skyscrapers based on the real world can easily be made compared to large Sci-Fi worlds that are purely from imagination. The player can easily decide if they want to re-create their life in this setting or try to become a version of themselves that they have always wanted, with lots of money, cars, and clothes. What if you want to make the world a better place? *Animal Crossing* might be set in a campsite or allows you to travel to a new city, but urban and rural settings are a perfect combination to create a new world or live a calm and peaceful life with your neighbors.

Seems familiar? Lots of these worlds are featured in games that you can buy on the shelf of your local video game shop. But what if you cannot decide on an environment for your game? What if a few different ones come to mind but you cannot decide which one you like best? Why not mix and match! There is nothing wrong with mixing them up as lots of games have regions that the player can explore. *Lego Marvel Superheroes 2* did this perfectly by creating a world that is made up of different worlds from famous comics, such as New York, Asgard, Egypt, Avengers Mansion, Wild West, and many more. Sometimes, choosing one environment may not be enough! Just be sure that if you decide to use more than one, have a good level of detail and ensure that there is a justified reason you have chosen to have multiple environments for your story.

Tutorials

How do players learn about the controls and abilities? Sometimes, it might be through experimentation, but it is typically through tutorial levels at the start of the game. Some games are detailed and guide the player slowly through their mechanics, some will leave the player to learn by themselves, or some will be a mixture of both.

Star Wars Jedi: Fallen Order is a perfect example of training the player how to carry out new abilities and learning the controls of the game (without giving away many spoilers!). The game begins with the player having to reach the top of a structure. But the player is given a lot of negative space to move. Perfect, now the player can use the left stick to move around. But the player needs to move forward to reach a ledge to progress to the goal. Once reached, we would instinctively press X or A to jump, but this teaches the player without giving much direction other than simply using previous skills from other games and hand placements on the chosen peripheral.

As you progress through the first level, the player is faced with their first round of enemies and their trusty weapon. But unlike other combat tutorials, the player is given directions about how to complete combinations, but they cannot progress till they have demonstrated that they know how to complete them. During my first run through the game, I thought this was excellent as I sometimes struggle to remember all combinations during my first playthrough. I soon found myself on a runaway train with multiple enemies that I needed to practice my newfound skills on. However, I found myself facing the same two enemies repeatedly, and no matter how many times I was defeating them, they kept on coming. As it turns out, I wasn't completing the combination correctly or following the instructions. While this might have caused some confusion, I found that this was perfect as there was no way I could progress until I had mastered this new move. (I can now say that I have now completed this level and am now one with the force!)

Overall, this is a perfect method to ensure that the player is completing mechanics correctly but also tapping into their muscle memory and training the player how to play the game in the way you designed it.

When teaching, students will learn new skills as they progress through lessons, assignments, projects, courses, etc. They will always be given the chance to reflect and think about how they would use their newfound skills differently in the future. Level design is used similarly to this, as you can give the player a chance to use their new skills if they visit a level, world, cave, temple, etc. again. Lots of open-world games will require the player to revisit old locations for things that they might have missed. In our case, using new abilities in previously restricted or locked locations is perfect for those that wish to grab all collectibles or anything they might have missed during their previous playthrough. I find that this is an excellent design method, as this allows the player the chance to appreciate the world you have designed, but to also make them feel that they are getting everything for their money. As we have mentioned before, making the player feel they are getting their money's worth for a game is important, as there is one crucial thing that a designer wants and that is for their game to sell!

However, when it comes to designing, the tutorial level tends to come last in production. It is argued that it is better to design the tutorial at the end once the mechanics have been designed fully so the tutorial can be designed correctly so the player can learn everything that the game has to offer. You could make the tutorial first, but you might find that once you make it, the design or style of the game might shift, which will result in you coming back to design the tutorial again to keep it in line with your game's design. Or don't have one at all and treat the entire game as a training level. You could teach the player new moves and mechanics, gaining new gear, experience new gameplay and keep them on their toes with what the game has to offer.

Let's Start Designing

With any great game come great environments, from roaring fields to vast, unexplored galaxies. There are worlds to be created for our players to explore. The only limit of creating a world is your imagination. But in the early days of video games, worlds did not start with 3D, so finding ways to make these worlds and levels could be quite tricky. Some early games you may have played had simple environments but soon turned into successful video games through the designing of their levels. As technology developed, so did the way we play games. This also meant that the way we see and interact with games did too. Fast forward to the present day, we are lucky to be able to experience stunning and expansive environments with our current technology, such as virtual reality.

Sometimes within game design, you may want to find ways to improve your workload and like something you have created so much that you want to give it more than one use. Why not reuse it? (Could it have more than fit into your game in other ways?) For those that may not have noticed, in the original *Super Mario Bros* World 1-1, you will notice that the images used for bushes and clouds are the same! The standard brick blocks are also used repeatedly and used in assorted colors in various levels. Back then, technology was limited so reusing assets was useful to help build worlds. But assets are not the only things that you can reuse, gameplay elements can also be used to help flesh out the game further. If you can make a gameplay element, such as shooting, running, stealth, climbing, driving, etc., be used more than a few times in your game, then it is worth keeping it. Having elements or systems like these in your game gives it diversity. You can be clever about reusing systems like these and how you want them to feature within your game. Some might even be introduced into the game through the form of levels. In *Far Cry 6* or *Grand Theft Auto V*, missions will be based around new vehicles or mechanics for the player to practice with and understand. This might also be a fantastic way to introduce the player to a certain user interface (UI) element and what it means and how to read it.

It is one thing to create a world for your players to explore in, but it is something else to make it engaging and exciting. Rather than it being static, you need to make it interactable and allow the player the drive to explore. The more exploring you provide, the better the chance to appreciate the world you have created and enjoy it in its entirety. This should be their playground while learning how to move from task to task while avoiding obstacles and immersing themselves in the story you have designed.

We have mentioned a lot of games through this book so far, and all of them have some expansive environments. Here are a few that have been mentioned so far:

- *GTA V*

- *Legend of Zelda: Breath of the Wild*

- *No Man's Sky*

- *Minecraft*

- *Ratchet & Clank: Rift Apart*

- *Marvel's Spider-Man*

- *The Elder Scrolls* series

While considering the preceding examples, we also need to take note of the genre of games they are. For example, *The Elder Scrolls* series are all medieval, which means the assets created for them must have a theme. This is something you are going to need to consider while making your environment.

Ever played a level and thought

- When will this end?!

- That was quick!?

When thinking about your levels or world, you need to think about the length of time it will take to complete the level. Of course, during the design stage, enemies and traps will come in after you have thought through a floor plan. When building your level, place your character at the start and see how long it takes to travel to the end. Time is going to be your friend here, as working out how long you want your level to be is crucial to determine the overall game runtime. There is nothing worse than for a player to have the thoughts that I just mentioned, which is why you want to keep things interesting through the means of traps, enemies, puzzles, story, mechanics, etc. Keeping the player on their toes during this will stop them from having the chance to think about time in the level. But try to avoid keeping the player going through some intense action scenes or emotional cutscenes continuously. Try to consider breaking everything up into chunks so they can feel like they can pause the game and come back to it later if they need to (but if they're really enjoying your game, they will never want to put it down!). Try not to wear the player out!

Immersive Environments

Being able to explore the world or levels through different times of the day will help give the player a real feel of travelling. They could be traversing a snowy cliff face or exploring a desert through scorching sunshine. How will the weather affect gameplay and how the player travels? What will the world around the player look like at night or when it's raining? Weather can also be used to represent mood. Maybe there has been a tragic death scene or a sunrise over a great victory. You can be as clever as you like with this, but make sure that all things connect! This also goes for getting the player to explore inside and the outside world. Having a variety of space such as interior and exterior stops the game from feeling the same. Giving the player an objective to move from an open world into a base or building or vice versa helps break things up, but make sure that this all feels natural. Having wider spaces can make the player feel safer but can also mean that you can throw some larger enemies or a big group of smaller enemies in there to give the player a challenge. Or having a tighter or small space to give a more dangerous feel. You might also want to add in a one-on-one battle in a narrower space.

Movement

Rather than moving around left to right, why not move up? Adding height to your world adds character but also gives the player a chance to practice mechanics. It also makes the world feel natural. What games have you played that have always stayed at the same level? Probably not many! By making a player climb to something or move up, it makes them feel that they are progressing to a goal. But what goes up can also come down. Giving the chance to explore something that is below the player continues to expand the world and prompts them to further their explorations to new areas in search of hidden items or collectibles. But some players might also want to jump off of heights to skip animations or speed up their gameplay time; this is where you can decide to add in fall damage if they choose to do this. If a player can jump from heights, be sure to allow the camera to show the player their true height; there is nothing more annoying than jumping down to something that looks like it can be reached and it ends up killing you. If you want the player to avoid doing this, why not add in other methods for their descent, such as ladders, platforms, lifts, or climbable surfaces. There's nothing more frustrating than finding something in the world that looks like it can be explored and then finding out that it is just there for show. Establishing a visual language in your game will help make sure that the player can determine the difference between somewhere that is explorable and something that is not. Some games use visuals or sounds to determine this. The earlier games in the *Pokémon* series used a thud sound to determine whether a player can venture past an object. Other games might use low bushes, rocks, and walls that tell the player that they are at the edge of the map or if this area is impassable. Having invisible walls removes the illusion that your world is alive; be sure to avoid this!

Before making your levels, it is always handy to make box levels to know where the placement of objects, vehicles, and hideaways will be. Box levels are empty spaces that will act as the framework for your level. Think of this as your playground and you are now deciding on where you would like to put everything. This level won't feature in your game but will simply be used to decide on your surroundings and will act as a testing ground for your mechanics and hazards. Both need to be tested and tweaked here to ensure that they work as intended and designed. This is what you need to consider when making your own box level:

- Don't make your ground flat. Add some height and gradient to it to test running and walking. This will help test your mechanics and animations to ensure that all runs smoothly and also that it looks good.

- Stack some objects on top of each other to test jumping and climbing. Think about the length and height geometry to test any double jumps or wall runs you might want to include.

- Test all mechanics and hazards to ensure the distance, timing, and how lethal they might be to the player. If they don't kill the player, then they might not be working!

What about combat? Is the player going to fight anything in your world? If so, then you need to create an area to test this. A combat arena is perfect for this, to allow tests on combat systems and enemies. When testing, find a way to have enemies spawn quickly and work with combinations of enemies to create fun and difficulty.

Alternate Pathways

When thinking about box levels, you want to think about how the player will explore your world. We have spoken before about movement and avoiding the player from walking far too much as this can become tiresome and boring. But to complement the different methods of travel we have mentioned before, why not think about different pathways the player can take to achieve their goal? When I say pathways, I mean the different routes that the player can take. Some games use a linear approach with there being only one route the player can take or give the option, and certain routes will include treasure or danger. Genres such as first-person, role-playing games (RPGs), or driving games require paths to avoid the game from being boring. But if you choose to make paths in your game, which one will the player choose? How can you entice the player to go down a certain path? Will one be more dangerous than the other, but have greater rewards? Will one be shorter than the other? Make sure that one pathway will be more significant than the other. Will you allow the player to backtrack and visit the other path at a later date?

When talking about backtracking and visiting previous places, some might find this boring and tedious; I feel the opposite. Being able to revisit somewhere makes you feel like you are getting the most out of the world and the game. Wouldn't you like someone to get the most out of your work? However, if this is something that you encourage, try to avoid making the player travel back and forth multiple times as this is when boredom can sneak in. If you decide that the player needs to visit a place more than once or twice, why not make it slightly different, so they feel that they are seeing something new? On the other hand, you should think about other ways that the player can move around the world and your level. These can be unlocked once the player has explored more of the world. The *Lego Star Wars* games are a great example as certain characters will be able to unlock doors, retrieve collectibles, and complete objectives that couldn't be completed until they had been unlocked. What if fast-travel or a vehicle couldn't be unlocked until the game has been completed? This gives the player a reason to come back and revisit a level or the game again once the main story or objective has been achieved. If you are going to include modes of transport, make sure that the player isn't using them all the time; otherwise, it can make your level feel long and boring. As we have mentioned before, make the experience different and diverse. If you ever feel that your level is long or boring, then it probably is. Adding variety into your level can avoid this and keep the player on their toes. If your player is travelling in one direction, why not add dead ends that have enemies or collectibles at the end of them? This encourages exploration and makes it feel fuller and deeper. This is also an easy way of building out your levels without it being too complex. It expands the life of your level and extends your playtime which is what you want. Don't ever let your player feel that they are zipping through your game too quickly! That being said, try to have something at the end of these dead ends; if your player explores a few of them but with no reward, they will quickly get bored and not explore anymore. Have something at the end of them, even if it is something they can destroy so they get some achievement out of being there. While doing this in your box levels, it allows you to experiment and test what works for you and the feel of the game.

Mapping

When exploring your world, how will the player keep track of where they have been? Most games will have some way of tracking their whereabouts around the world or have a compass to guide them. Having a map to keep track of this is a perfect way to do so. Some games even provide maps in their game boxes for the player as a souvenir. *Grand Theft Auto* and *The Elder Scrolls* series were known for this so the player could put the map on their wall or follow their progress physically as an added touch. When designing a map, this is crucial to show yourself and the design team how the different areas of the game will connect and relate to each other. Where do you want the player to travel? What direction do you want them to take? Will there be secret pathways? Where do you want items to be hidden? These are all things that will be shown on your world design but not on the players of course! One thing I love to read are the walk-through books that come with games. They help show levels and areas of the game that the player can explore to sneak past enemies and find hidden items and are the best way to see how the levels have been designed. It is like taking a sneak peek into a designer's head and seeing what they were thinking about during the design phase. But what if your game does not have a need for a map? How do you show progression? *Super Smash Bros* use a method of unlocking characters the more you play. As you progress through the World of Light mode, characters would be unlocked in your roster until you have everyone to play as. Characters could then be purchased within a DLC expansion. But players could tell that they have completed the main segment of the game when they have unlocked all the fighters.

But what if you can see the end of the game or where the player will end up? *The Legend of Zelda: Breath of the Wild* shows you where you need to travel to for the final mission of the game. Hyrule Castle is set in the center of the world, so wherever you travel, you will always see your destination as you move the camera round. This can also be seen from the highest points in the world, just to remind the player that this will be their final objective. This is an excellent method as the player will always know where they need to go, but also shows that if they get too close to the destination before they are ready, they will encounter enemies that are too strong to defeat. This is a perfect way to deflect any daring players who think they can finish the game before they experience everything!

Once you have thought about what you would like to feature in your world, now you need to think about the WHY. Although you have a story that you want your players to enjoy, how does the story reflect in the world? Your world needs to have a purpose for the player to explore it. The reason for this is called a goal. A goal should be a reason for your player to explore the world and make them want to venture out into what you have designed. Here are a few ideas of goals that you could set for your world that the player could complete or experience:

- Idea 1 – What if your player was put somewhere that they didn't need to be? Sometimes, venturing too far into something can be the best way to create action, tense atmospheres, and location by putting them somewhere that could create danger for them. If they can survive or struggle with this area, would they want to come back again when they are feeling stronger?

- Idea 2 – As we have mentioned, exploring is one of the best goals for an environment. By letting the player venture on their own, they can create their own feel for the story and experience things at their own pace. Being able to let players venture out into the world you have made is one of the most satisfying things to feel as a designer. If they love the world you have made, then you can sleep happily knowing you set out what you wanted to achieve!

- Idea 3 – As someone in education, I cannot say that I have seen many educational games made. This is due to the stigma of educational games being for "young people" or "not cool." But there are ways of being able to educate players through games and their story. The *Uncharted* series teaches the players about some of the history of Nathan Drake and the famous pirate Henry Avery. While the history of these icons was altered to fit the game's story, the background and why they became famous was taught to the player so they could understand who they were. This is partly why I enjoyed these games so much due to the historical element to them as I love history and what came before!

- Idea 4 – We have spoken about morals before, but what if they were tested in the game? (Spoiler inbound!) At the end of *Grand Theft Auto V*, the player is given three choices, kill either of the two supporting characters or the "deathwish option." This gave the player the chance to think about their morals and what impact they want to have on the rest of their playtime. You can use choice or consequence to deliver the final moral goal for the game or level. This choice will impact the gameplay for either the rest of the game or for the final cutscene.

In larger open-world games, the player is given the chance to explore the world in their own time or through the means of the story. *Grand Theft Auto V* is perfect for this as the game will begin in the main city of Los Santos, the playground for most of the game's story. As the player progresses, they are encouraged to explore further into the world, thus giving the illusion that the world is much bigger than they first expected. Once far enough into the game, they are transported to a new location in the world to now explore there. This then introduces the player to flying vehicles so they can move around the world in new ways. This keeps the gameplay diverse and moves away from land vehicles. Eventually, the player is tasked to chase some cars around the main road of the map, thus completing a full circuit and seeing most of the world in one mission. While the player carries out these tasks, the areas of the map are revealed in the start menu. Only by exploring the map in full using all modes of transport can the player find any easter eggs and hidden weapons.

A good example to consider is *The Elder Scrolls: Skyrim* as this does a good job of encouraging the player to explore the world around them. Although this map is much larger than *GTA V*, it follows a similar method of letting the player explore the world through story-based missions. However, there is no possible way to explore the map in its entirety just by playing the story; the player will either need to complete side quests or venture out on their own. A common feature for large open-world games is to give the player the option to fast-travel to previously visited locations. While this might seem obvious to veteran gamers, this is a really useful feature to include if you are thinking of having a larger world for your player. Think back to the movement and getting the player through the levels; if you have a large map, will the player spend most of it on foot? Or will you provide ways to travel across the world?

Player Controls

What is a game if you can't play it? One of the most important things to playing a game is knowing HOW to play it – whether this is down to the instructions that come with a board game or down to the way to press buttons on your keyboard or controller. Either way, the player needs to know the best way to play the game and if the way you have decided the player needs to be played is possible. Sounds simple? But button mapping is crucial when working with controls for a game. Again, sounds simple. But the designing of this takes time and care.

With this in mind, we now need to think about ergonomics, which is the study of equipment fitting with the worker, or in our case, how the controller or keyboard will work with our player. When designing controls, you need to consider the placement of a player's hands. For example, a first-person shooter typically has the player's hand on the mouse and the other on the WASD keys. You'll notice that when you go to watch someone play on a PC, their hands will land in that position without thinking about it. You'll notice that this also happens when picking up a controller, your fingers tend to land on the triggers or bumpers, left thumb on the left stick and the right thumb onto the A or X key. Funny, isn't it? It's muscle memory and shows our hands are ready to play! (This is also down to the comfortability for the player.) As the player progresses further into the game, they start to learn and remember the controls you created. Over time, they start to associate the muscle movement to the controls without even knowing.

When thinking about a keyboard and a controller, designers tend to give every button on a controller a function, but you don't need to do that for a keyboard. The last thing you want is to give a function to all 26 letters on a keyboard, as it can soon become too much! Keeping the controls localized and near each other, you'll soon see that your game becomes easy to play and comfortable for the player. If your game requires the player to take their hands off the mouse to reload their gun while aiming, you'll soon see that your player is typing rather than playing!

But what can you do to design your controls? Look at some of the following tips:

- Ever thought about making games for a younger audience? Think about those small hands that might be holding a typical sized controller or trying to reach their fingers for buttons on a keyboard. Try to keep button functions simple and close together. Also, think about combinations of buttons; will a child be able to remember or react quick enough to press keys for an action?

- Everyone loves a fighting game and going head-to-head with a friend or the computer. But these games are notorious for creating complex combinations to pull off some amazing attacks. I can't say that I have played many fighting games in my time (mine were always the DC *Injustice* series), but I still can't master quick combinations to defeat my enemies (it might just be down to my reflexes!). Don't get me wrong, I love a fighting game as much as the next gamer, but be sure to think about the combinations that need to be carried out and how likely the player will be able to complete them.

- What about offering the player some control over their controls? Sometimes, a player prefers to use a southpaw method or even something new. Giving the player some control over how they play the game is always helpful, especially when it comes to accessibility options (something that will be covered in a later chapter).

- When moving in a vehicle, are you wanting to give a realistic or simplistic control scheme? In the good old days of playing racing games such as *Need for Speed* on the Game Boy Advance, acceleration was carried out when holding down the A button while the R button was braking or reversing. Fast forward to today, it can be the other way around. The right trigger might be to accelerate, and the A button might be to use a handbrake. The more buttons you have, the more creative you can be.

I have mentioned this briefly before about not knowing what to do at the start of a game, or even in the middle of a game, but there have been times where I didn't know what to do in a level, so I hit every button there was on the controller! This was with the hope that something might happen! But this needs to be avoided at all costs, as the last thing you want is for your player to feel confused about what they do next or if they forget the controls. Don't let the player resort to button mashing! Unless it's a fighting game, and you may end up pulling off that awesome move that you didn't think was possible, then you can thank me later! But then you might want to push all the buttons again to find out what the combination is that you pressed to pull off that move.

What if you have a button that does nothing? What will be the point in having it at all? Will you have the player remove the button when they're not using it? Of course not! Never have a button rendered useless or not used. There may be times where the player might not be able to shoot as they are out of ammo, so what do you want the shoot button to do? Will it play a noise to indicate that you have no ammo? Will pressing it make the player switch weapons to one that has ammo? Will you have buttons and abilities unlocked over time? In some tutorials, the player has to progress far enough into a game before they can use a button or a combination of buttons. Just remember to teach the player a new move in turn, not to have them being taught all at once. This can get very confusing!

What is the next best thing to a button? An analog stick! This useful little stick is the foundation for so many mechanics in all manner of games and is your best friend when it comes to playing. The best thing about this is that you get to play with two of them! Most typically known for movement, the left stick is perfect to replicate real-world action, whether it be directional or steering. The analog stick used to be used for simulators to create a realistic experience of piloting a vehicle. Now, we can use the smaller version of that same stick to move our character through the world or pilot a plethora of vehicles we see. A clever use of the stick is when the player needs to balance when walking across something. In *Uncharted: Drake's Fortune*, Nathan Drake must walk across a fallen tree which results in him having to keep his balance. At the time of the PS3, the console introduced motion into its controllers, but the player could either use this motion control or the stick to balance Nathan before he could plummet his way to death. The left stick is seen as the more diverse stick compared to its twin. The right stick is typically used as the camera controller to allow the player to look around the world or to aim a weapon or target. Sometimes, the left stick might be used to target a shot fired in some of the recent Lego Games. While holding down the shoot button (X or square if you're on a console), you can then move the target to where you would like to shoot. The right stick might also make an appearance if the player needs to complete a combination of moves or a mechanic, but it's safe to say that the left gets more action!

Back to the subject of buttons, what would you like them to do? I'm talking about the four buttons on the right side of your controller, ABXY for Xbox and Nintendo Switch or Cross, Square, Triangle, and Circle for PlayStation. The best example I can give when thinking about different character moves or abilities is the *Lego Star Wars* games. In my opinion, I feel that these are some of the easiest game controls in all the games I have played. The controls are as follows (for Xbox and PlayStation):

- Left stick – Movement

- X/A – Jump/double jump

- Circle/B – Force ability or holstering of weapon

- Triangle/Y – Change character or enter vehicle

- Square/X – Attack

Notice how the control pad (the arrow keys on a controller, also known as a D-pad) and the right stick don't make an appearance? They don't in earlier *Lego Star Wars* entries, but more recent games have included the right stick with more open-world environments and added the use of the bumpers to change character. But the concept of moving the character and using the basic buttons makes the games very easy to play and pick up after years of not playing. But what happens if the player needs to use two buttons at the same time? And what if they are with the same thumb? Madness! But *Spider-Man PS4* uses this method to use a supercharged attack when building up enough attack combinations. This means the player needs to press circle and triangle at the same time to deliver this special attack. This is a common method to use but make sure that the player has the reach for the buttons. If you are making them press the triangle, left trigger, and down on the D-pad while also moving forward and aiming up, it will confuse the player and make this impossible to attempt. Feel free to try it, but you might find that you'll struggle! Simple and memorable is how you need to design controls. Make sure that the player can reach them but also achievable!

The last thing to think about for your controller is the vibrations. With the way technology and how we play games has evolved, the way we feel games and how they respond to us has also changed. In recent years, a controller has gone from just a simple shake in the player's hands to a situation where vibrations will reflect something that is happening progressively. For example, one of the earliest games I can remember playing where the vibrations felt that they were reflecting what was happening was a heartbeat sensor in *Call of Duty: Modern Warfare 2*. Being able to hide in a snowstorm while looking at the sensor to see if there was an enemy nearby was a clever use of vibrations. While I may not have been looking at the sensor all the time, the vibrations were able to help me tell whether someone was getting close. Vibrations can be your friend; if you can find a way to make them feel that they are responding to the player's actions, then you are onto a winner.

The PlayStation 5 brought in a new way to feel triggers and actions within a game. Sony introduced adaptive triggers to give the player the feeling that they were pulling on a real trigger or pressing down on an accelerator. If you ever find yourself developing for a PlayStation 5 and you have the option to incorporate this into your game, go for it! This is just my opinion however, but I think this feature is awesome!

Bonus Stage: The Name of the Game

In all the game design lessons I have been part of, this is one of the trickiest questions to ask my students. Some projects my students make do not end up with names and have placeholders, or the placeholder's name became the name of the game. While this can be a fun process or activity to think about, it can sometimes be tricky to think of a name. I tend to tell my students that the name will come later in development and that there is no harm to pitch a game with no name yet.

But what about the naming of levels? As we have previously spoken about, games will use chapters or levels to show the player progressing through the game and story, but these may also have names to give the player an insight into what is yet to come. When thinking about the naming of your levels/chapters, have a think about the following:

- Numbers – Simple and effective, it keeps the player informed of the progression of the game. This was the typical way to show the player that they were progressing through the game. *Super Mario* used this with World 1-1. The player could tell that they were moving through worlds and levels, but they would never know how many levels there were until they completed the game. It also lacks personality by only giving a number.

- Location – Sometimes, naming the level after the place the level is set can be the best way to tell the player where they are located. Although this has its benefits, it may not always be what the player thinks. You could call a level Police Station, but have the location stormed by enemies. Look at what happened in *Batman: Arkham Knight* when Gotham PD was surrounded (spoilers!).

- Chapter names – A common method for games to use while treating the game like a novel. Sometimes, using chapter titles such as Endgame, The End, or From Small Beginnings can be ominous and keep the player guessing. You can be creative with this method, but the names are not always remembered, and the levels are referred to by their gameplay.

Why not be clever with your level titles? Some designers like to leave hints within their level titles to foreshadow something. *Dead Space* used this method and left a hidden message using the first letter of every level! I will leave you to play the game to find that message!

Conclusion

So far within this chapter, we have covered the following:

1. What do you need to consider when designing a level?

2. Control setup and what makes a game easy to play through a controller

3. Designing your game's world

4. Mapping your game through the world and levels

With another chapter now complete, we can now start to think about filling your game world with enemies. What will they look like? How will they be defeated? But more importantly, what is their purpose? All of these will be considered as we reach the halfway point of the book!

CHAPTER 6

Friend or Foe? Enemy Design

We have covered characters, environments, controls, levels, and a few handy tips and tricks to get you started. But what are the obstacles the player might face? Or better still, what will try to kill the player? Granted, not every game has something that will want to kill the player, but this will depend on your idea and how they fit into your world. But not all enemies are generated by the computer, some might be human competitors through multiplayer. This chapter will help us consider the basics when it comes to designing an enemy for our player and the sort of obstacles that we can create.

Where Do You Begin?

Designing an enemy is very much like designing your main character or a side character; all enemies must have a purpose. I have seen many a game where enemies will simply move from side to side and show no real character or personality. Of course, the main function there was to add difficulty for the player, but that was it. They did not chase after you, they did not shoot at you, it all seemed very static (which is a word that will be used a lot more as we move through this chapter). But what aspects do you need to think of when designing an enemy? Here are some characteristics to consider:

- Size
- Behavior
- Speed
- Movement
- Attacks
- Health

M. Killick, *The Way We Play*, https://doi.org/10.1007/978-1-4842-8789-7_6

Before you begin to draw your enemy and think of the preceding list, you need to think about the function of your enemy. While you may be sitting there thinking of a design in your head or drawing it on paper, you need to think about how it will be programmed: Will it be tricky to rig? How will it be textured? Will it be achievable? With these characteristics and your level's theme, you will be able to determine who your enemies are and how they will interact with the world around them. If you design a good enemy once, you will not need to design them again!

Size

Let us think about the first characteristic on the list, size. No game has the same size or types of enemies throughout; every game will have a variety that will put your skills to the test, but to also range in difficulty. How many different enemies are there in *Super Mario*? Or *Rayman*? Or *Call of Duty*? Or *Final Fantasy*? The list goes on! Some enemies might be reused or improved in sequels, but the ethos will always be the same. Here is a list of sized enemies to consider:

- Short – Enemies are not taller than the player's waist. Even when Super Mario is at his smallest form, Goombas are still shorter than him!

- Average – Enemies are of similar height as the player. These tend to be an even match for the player but can also still provide a challenge.

- Large – Much taller than the average enemy and will require wit and skill to defeat. Can be twice the player's height.

- Huge – Up for the challenge? An enemy that can be a struggle to be seen wholly on your screen and may require ranged attacks to ensure its defeat.

The size of the enemy will determine how the player will fight it. Smaller enemies might require a melee attack, which will also preserve ammo for the larger enemies. Much larger enemies might require skilled attacks and a range of high and low attacks. Work with the height of the player and the enemy; there is nothing more boring than hitting an enemy in the same place compared to hitting a creature in various places! But size can also have an influence on health. Typically, the larger the enemy, the greater the health, and it will be harder to kill. Size will also determine the reaction to projectiles and being hit. Smaller enemies might fly backward or flinch and then retaliate, and a larger enemy might not react to a hit at all. Having a variety of sizes can also help influence the player's emotions and prevent boredom. For example, if a player can defeat a huge enemy, then they may feel empowered and heroic for taking down a difficult foe, and defeating a group of smaller enemies without taking a hit might make you feel like a badass. You will always hear someone in your life say, "Size never matters!" When it comes to game design, the size of the enemy will always matter!

Behavior

Thinking back to the list of characteristics, the next one to consider is behavior. This refers to a few things:

- How does the enemy move around the world/level?

- What does the enemy do when it faces conflict?

- What does it do when it is hurt?

Sounds simple? If you create an enemy that follows these simple steps, then you will have something robust. But there are several types of enemies which all depend on their movement and behaviors, and enemies work best when they complement each other.

- Patroller – One of the simplest enemies to make and featured in some of the earliest video games such as *Pac-Man* and *Super Mario*. These simply move left, right, up, and down, and their movements are predictable.

- Chaser – These will pursue the player if approached or spotted. They might start as patrollers before changing to a chaser state if a condition is met by the player, which will result in the enemies attacking the player if close contact is made.

- Shooter – Quite simply, an enemy that will shoot at the player. These can both be chasers and patrollers but will shoot at the player once attacked. They will also keep their distance when shooting the player unless the player gets too close.

- Guard – An enemy that will protect something from the player but will only pursue the player for a certain distance to ward them off. These might be stronger enemies to give the player a challenge to collect a protected item.

- Flyer – An enemy that flies, simple as that. These give dimension to the game rather than fighting enemies on the ground. These can swoop down and attack the player, or they can shoot at them, or both!

- Teleporter – One that can change position around the battlefield. These can be quick but will require skill to stop them before they move again. Think of ways the player might be able to disable their movements long enough to stop them.

- Blocker – They will defend themselves through the means of a shield or a defensive device. Shields can be destroyed or temporarily disabled to allow the player to make their attacks. Sometimes, shields may need recharging and will leave them defenseless and open to an attack.

The reason for having a varied number of behaviors is to allow the player to work with their mechanics and skills to defeat any obstacles they face. This also allows the enemies to complement each other with their behaviors to create varied gameplay and creative puzzles. While the player explores their world and encounters enemies, this then teaches them about threat levels. This makes the player question: Which will be the easiest one to kill? Or what is the best way to approach this?

But what enemies work well with each other? Here are a few combinations you could work with:

- Blocker and shooter – The player might want to defeat the shooter while the blocker is defending them. Take out the vulnerable first!

- Patrollers and flyer – A ground and aerial assault for the player. Decide if the air support will create more of a problem and then deal with the easier enemies, or defeat the flyer at a distance and pick off the patrollers one by one.

- Teleporter and guard – While you are trying to defeat a guard, an enemy might be darting around you to stop your attacks.

- Chaser and patroller – The player might be open to chaser attacks while defeating the patrollers.

As the player progresses through the game, the speed and size of enemies might become more erratic and difficult. This could make them harder to kill and become a challenge.

Speed

But enemies or hazards don't always have to be chasing you; the difference between them can simply be mobility. In lots of shooter games, you may find turrets set up to defend certain areas or other enemies. But these can rotate and target the player and are still classed as an enemy. This also goes for a humongous creature that has limited or no mobility but can still be classed as an enemy. Make sure that you design your enemies that can keep the player engaged and decide their plan of attack. They might want to defeat any turrets or defenses before they take on any mobile enemies. Making the player think of a strategy will always keep them on their toes!

The next thing to consider when designing an enemy is the speed. You might have seen faster enemies have lower health, and slower enemies will take more damage to defeat. But finding the balance between fighting a computer and the game feeling realistic is where true mastery in design takes place. Ensuring that you are creating the illusion that the player is fighting a real enemy and needing to use strategy to defeat them creates the atmosphere that is needed when playing a game. But what is the best way to design the speed of enemies?

Slow enemies are perfect when there are a group of them. Most zombie games will incorporate a varied list of zombies to defeat based on size and speed. In most *Call of Duty: Zombies* modes, the first few waves feature a small group of slow-moving enemies to give the player a chance to explore the environment and choose a vantage point for future rounds. The zombies don't feel very threatening and can be easily beaten. But getting cornered by slow movers could lead to your defeat! Slow movers can be intimidating! But the further the player progresses, the speed and size gradually increases, thus increasing the difficulty.

Fast enemies are somewhat the trickiest to defeat and require fast finger movements to stop them. These can dart forward and attack as soon as they are engaged. They tend to work best in horror and action games. The best way to defeat them is with skill and learning. Ever been killed by the same enemy multiple times? Ever thought about how they move and what their fighting pattern is? Sometimes, the best way to learn is to die! Learning the move patterns of a fast enemy through repetition might be the best way to overcome them. Or if you are are a pro-gamer and quick with blocking and attacking and defeating them without dying, then they won't be a problem for you! Again, thinking of size, a smaller enemy might be the quickest and have an erratic move pattern, which could prove a challenge for your player.

Movement

As mentioned, some enemies will be quicker than the player, which will mean they need to act quickly to counter or avoid an attack. Try giving your player a prompt and have an attack indicator above the enemy; this will give the player the correct timing to dodge or parry an attack. But what about the rest of their movement style? How will they travel around the environment? What will they do once you are spotted? And what do they do if they spot threats that aren't the player? Showing your understanding of these will not only determine their attacks but also their personality.

You need to consider whether your enemies will move randomly or in a set pathway. There's nothing worse than to see enemies moving in the set pathway that doesn't seem or feel realistic. Try to include a variety of move styles that give the illusion that they are meant to be part of the world you are making. Stormtroopers are the perfect example when it comes to the personality of enemies in *Star Wars Jedi: Fallen Order*. While they will react to you once spotted, they will move in packs and patrol the area like soldiers would and from the films. Some groups of enemies might flank the player or even flock together to box the player in. This is when things get tight, and the player needs to think on their toes about how to get out of tight situations. While this might focus on humanoid enemies, what about animals? Lots of games that focus on exploring maps in the wild and uncharted spaces will feature animals from the real world. This is where behavioral patterns come into play. Consider how animals, insects, fish, and birds move for reference. While humans and humanoids will walk in straight lines, predators might move in arcs to circle their prey, and birds will circle and swoop down to attack.

Whether you are working in a team to create a game or working on your own, there are a few questions you need to answer when it comes to programming enemy movements and their behavior:

- What is their movement like? Can they jump over obstacles or hide from any shots you fire? Do they slide into cover?

- What is their aggression like? Do they cower with fear or take you on headfirst? Some enemies like to run and hide, and some like to sneak up on you and take you from behind. Thinking about this will help them seem realistic and relative to the world around them.

- Some games allow enemies to pick up weapons or items from fallen teammates. How clever/desperate are they when it comes to combat? Will they drive vehicles into you or away from you? Some enemies might control turrets if another was killed manning it. What is their behavior like based on other enemies?

- What will they do to defend themselves? Will they use shields and get in close to the player? Will their moves be stealthy or erratic? Will they cover another enemy while another sets up equipment to beat you?

- Will they raise an alarm if they spot you? What will their reaction be? Do they come in pairs and carry out grouped attacks? Does the final enemy flee once they see their teammates defeated?

When it comes to designing the enemies, most games will use pathways to determine where the enemies will move to and what animations will play during that. For example, if an enemy walks a certain path, then an animation might play showing the enemy looking over a cliff or edge before walking away. This, in turn, might give the player a chance to pull the enemy off the edge! But these enemies will walk around a certain path following invisible waypoints or markers to make them look like they're patrolling an area. With this in place, you can design the world around them, such as necessary hiding spots, objects that could be blown up, etc. If this is the method you choose, ensure that movement is smooth and doesn't clip any surrounding areas and play around with what works for your game and enemies!

Attacks

What is the point of having an enemy in your game that you can't defeat or fight back? As we continue to think about the designing of your enemies, we need to think about how the player will combat them.

In earlier games such as *Super Mario*, enemies would appear on the screen as you moved further through the level, giving no indication on what they can do and what abilities they might have and giving no real introduction to them. However, some games such as *Space Invaders* had a short animation for the enemies to appear on the screen. At times, some space invaders would fall to the bottom of the screen toward the player to defeat them. But again, there was no real introduction into these enemies; it was more of a see-and-shoot scenario. Considering enemies' introductions is an excellent way for the player to gauge a feel for the enemies and what challenge they might face. It is also a great way for the player to know that they are entering a battle or even knowing that they have found a foe. Here are a few tips to think about:

- If you're thinking cinematically, you could freeze the camera on the enemy so the player can spot any weaknesses. It can be fun to give the player a chance to experiment attacks and learn weaknesses of the enemy, but it can also be great for the player to come up with a strategy from the first impression the player has.

- Someone giving an enemy a name the player can refer to, adds personality to the creature to person they are about to kill.

- In *The Last of Us* series, clickers are notorious for being dangerous and difficult to kill. But the player can tell when they are near one by the sound of their frightening clicking noise. Creating tension by the sound of an enemy that the player has learned is a challenge to kill is a perfect way to keep the player ready for anything. It's also a great use of foreshadowing to let them know that danger is right around the corner.

- First impressions are hard to erase, so why not do that with your enemies? Give them a dramatic entrance that the player will never forget! In *Mortal Kombat*, the player and foe throw quips at each other and introduce each other with a badass monologue. Think about how you want your enemy to be perceived from the first encounter with the player.

It's one thing to think about the entrance of the enemy, but how they spawn into the world is another. Depending on the genre of game you plan to make, this will help determine how the enemies will appear. If you are making a Sci-Fi game, then enemies might appear through teleports or land from the sky in pods that the player will need to avoid. You can be savvy with entrances but also turn them into a challenge for the player. Enemies might also climb over walls or climb out of the ground. These methods make them feel more realistic but also avoid the whole "spawning out of nowhere" scenario which can look a bit dry and not very creative.

Thinking about the way enemies appear in the world also gives the player a chance not to slay all of their enemies before they make their way onto the screen. There is nothing worse than defeating all of your enemies at once. This skips all fun you might have designed and makes the game feel too easy. Or consider the enemies spawning off-screen and run toward the player. This is a perfect way to catch the player off guard and deliver an unexpected attack!

In spite of all of this, there should be one crucial thing to consider when designing combat for enemies: it should be fun! If you are designing an action game where a core element of it is fighting enemies, then it should be fun to play! But you can design this in whatever way you like. You can have explosions, humorous dialogue from the enemies when they are wounded, or gory victory kills. But make it worth the player's while and reward them for achieving gory kills or pulling off that special combo of moves or a weapon that will make the next kill all the more satisfying. Giving the player a reason to go charging into battle and feeling like they will get something out of it gives them that incentive to risk using their limited health or ammo for something that will assist them greatly on their quest. In *Dying Light*, the player has the chance to find the legendary sword of Excalibur after defeating the enemies guarding it. Once achieved, the player can swim to the rocks where they can retrieve the weapon. This is the perfect reward and provides a perfect advantage against the onslaught of zombies in the game.

What happens when an enemy is defeated? Will it burst into flames and ash? Will it turn to bones and dust? Will it leave anything behind that can be claimed? Will they go down screaming dramatically? Will you have your enemies explode and try to damage the player before they leave? It's good to think about an entrance for an enemy, but their exit also needs to be just as strong. The Elites in the *Halo* series have their iconic scream to tell the player they have been defeated. Make their exits one that helps tell the player that they have been successful in their fight. Think about how the game will change once an enemy is defeated. Sometimes, an enemy will drop items such as experience points that will help the player level up their gameplay experience or level up weapons or in-game currency that can be used to buy that bigger weapon the player wants to use, or the enemy will stay there and remind the player of their victory. Sometimes, the enemy's bodies will stay in the world for the rest of the game to remind the player of where they have been.

When it comes to playing any game that has enemies, they are meant to be fought, not avoided. Why? Because they were put there for a reason. Whether for fun or for the challenge and reward. Ever played a game and thought: "Those enemies are too easy to kill and won't give me much of a reward if I kill them. So, I'm better off just running past them." When designing a game, you want your players to fight every time. If the player starts skipping enemies and combat, then they are clearly bored or in a rush to beat the game. Both scenarios must be avoided! Remember, you want your player to have fun and get the most out of the price they paid for your game. If they are going to invest x-number of hours into your game, then you want them to feel rewarded for killing every enemy they see. Give them a reason for risking their life to fight their enemies. Why not think about the following:

- Ammo, health, money, weapons? What makes them desirable? Make them fight for what they need and make them crush their enemies to get what they want!

- Do they stand in the way of something? If your path is blocked, could an enemy stand in your way to progressing? Or could it lead you on another quest to get past it? In some classic *Pokémon* games, the player would need an item to wake up a Snorlax to venture further. The player then has the choice to defeat the Pokémon or capture it!

- Similar to blocking your path, what if they have something you need to progress to another room or building? They could have an item that unlocks a door and takes you further on your quest.

- Thinking back to personalities for enemies, their dialogue is great for the setting of the game but to also add some humor. Grunts in *Halo* games are excellent for taunting the player and motivating them to fight them. Make them regret laughing or insulting you!

While you're defeating the enemies using your awesome attacks, what about the ways the enemies could defeat you? We have looked at the types of enemies you could design, but what about the ways they could defeat the player?

- Do they use weapons that fire projectiles? Do they shoot arrows or bullets? Can the player use whatever they use? How accurate will ranged attacks be? Your enemies might wait undercover and plan their attack for the perfect shot. When your enemies are reloading might be the perfect time to attack them!

- Swords or bats? Fists or kicks? Do they know martial arts? Will your enemies be using melee attacks?

- Does your enemy have an aftereffect? When they are defeated, do they leave a cloud of poison to incapacitate the player while they fight other enemies? Will they explode once defeated to have that last minute victory over the player?

Whatever you decide, think about how this can be animated and rigged by your team. Make sure that it is achievable!

Rather than attacks being spontaneous, give the player a chance to prepare/see when the enemy is about to attack. Having an animation to tell the player that they need to brace themselves for an attack is crucial when designing an enemy. The enemy could prepare to swing a sword or melee weapon, or cock back a gun, or pull the pin on a grenade. Either way, you need to have an indication that the enemy is ready for combat, and they are trying to engage with the player.

However, not every attack the enemy makes has to deal damage. If designing melee weapon combat, the enemy might block or parry. This could make the player stagger and defenseless for a short period of time before they can continue. This is an excellent way to break the flow of combat but also make the enemy look like they are a worthy opponent.

Some enemies might try to create distance between themselves and the player. In *Star Wars Jedi: Fallen Order*, when fighting Sith enemies, they will Force Push Cal away to engage in ranged attacks. This also gives the player a chance to think about a strategy and also heal themselves if they need to. Again, this breaks up the flow of combat and encourages the player to get back in there and carry on with the fight.

Sometimes, making the enemies fight similarly to you is a perfect way to make the player feel as if they have met their match. If you can stun, freeze, or halt your enemies, then they should be able to do it to you! While the enemies could be defenseless, this could also happen to you. You can't always feel like you're winning; otherwise, it would be too easy! In Square Enix's *Guardians of the Galaxy*, Peter Quill can use his elemental guns to freeze, stun, and pull his enemies. But the player can also be victim to the same attacks. If this is an option for you, be sure to give the player a chance to escape. They might need to repeatedly press a button to be unfrozen, or they could be incapacitated for a short period of time. But be sure to keep it short, any longer and it could become frustrating for the player.

If you can heal mid-fight, then why can't the enemy? If you plan to use this mechanic, be sure to use it infrequently to avoid the game feeling unfair. No matter the difficulty or size of the enemy, always give the player the feeling that they have the edge in battle. If your enemy is healing, you can add an animation to show they are. This might also be a chance for the player to deal damage while the enemy is healing if you decide to make this a vulnerable state.

Similar to healing, the enemy could buff their abilities for a short period of time. This will make them stronger or impervious to certain attacks. This might also give the chance for the player to step back and think about their next move. If this is something you are thinking about adding, why not think about how it could be stopped? The enemy could have a "buffing" animation play to tell the player that their enemy is getting stronger, before dealing damage during a vulnerable state. This could then reverse the enemy buffing and level the playing field.

What if you had your trusty weapon taken from you? The enemy could steal something from the player to give them the advantage. This changes the motive from "fight the enemy" to "Give me back my stuff!". Give the player a fair chance to get back what was stolen and not what was found through progression. If items can be stolen, make sure they are replaceable if they end up getting destroyed or damaged in battle.

Everything has a weakness, so your player should be able to exploit that. The *Pokémon* series is perfect to balancing moves and understanding what opponents' weaknesses are. For example, if you think that your opponent is using a Grass-type Pokémon, then they should be impervious to fire attacks. The player should be able to use logic to defeat their enemies and never feel that they are confused or feel that something doesn't work.

Health

Quite simply, how much damage can the enemy take before they are defeated? No matter the size or abilities an enemy might have, there must always be a way to defeat it. Determining the health of an enemy is calculated in the same way you would for the player. If you have an enemy toward the end of your game and the player has weapons that deal greatly in damage, then will you want your enemies to be defeated in one hit? Think about the ratio of damage dealt by the player at certain points in the game and the health the enemy will need to have. You wouldn't want an overpowered enemy at the start when the player has little or no weapons! You also need to think about the different attacks your player can deal and how effective they might be on your enemy. Will you have some enemies that can be defeated in one hit, or three? Just make sure that when you are deciding on the health of an enemy, they don't become bullet sponges. This is when the player can pump a silly amount of bullets into an enemy before they deal any real damage or defeat them. If your enemy has armor on, then make it clear visually on the enemy that the player will need to work harder to take them down. Always test this during your development stage and gather feedback based on how much health and damage an enemy has.

Your enemy might have a defense meter that will need to be drained before their health can be depleted. In *Star Wars Jedi: Fallen Order*, most Stormtroopers or bosses will have a defense meter under their health bar. This can be depleted through the use of parries or constant direct attacks. Once reduced to zero, the player can then deal damage that can reduce the enemy's health. This defense meter can be restored again, and the cycle continues until the player has won.

Honorable Mention: Buffs and Weaknesses

While the player might receive these from weapons or special abilities, your enemies might be at an advantage based on their environment. A buff is quite simply a boost and can give the advantage over someone or something else. If you are fighting an enemy in a volcano and they are made out of lava, then they might have a power buff based on their surrounding environment. In the *Pokémon* series, certain Pokémon will receive a buff to their abilities and moves based on the weather. If it is raining, then water-based Pokémon will be given a boost. However, this can also be played to the player's advantage. For example, if you are fighting an enemy in a volcano, then water-type moves or spells will be super effective against them. This also works for the enemy attacks made toward the player. So think about the environment the player is doing battle; let them find ways to take advantage of the area they are in!

Stuck with Ideas?

It can be very hard to come up with an original design for an enemy when there are so many games out there that may have already done every type of enemy under the sun. How many games have zombies or the undead? Or mercenaries? Gangsters?

Orcs? Witches and sorcerers? Although these might be your traditional enemies, you can always have a go at making your own. Here are a few things to think of if you take this route:

- Think about your theme and how your enemies could fit into your environment. If you are near a volcano, will you face off against molten lava creatures that spit magma at the player? Or evil snowmen that throw snowballs at you?

- Your story will have an impact in the way you design your game and the enemies within it. Sometimes, the enemies reflect the game's final boss. If your game has a giant mechanical robot as its final boss, then the player would expect to see robotic enemies to face off with.

- What if you have enemies that fight in similar ways to others? Why not reuse some of the animations you have for other enemies? If you have two enemies that are similar to each other, why not have them fight and move similarly to each other? Have some slight differentiation; otherwise, someone will think you're being lazy. I call it being clever!

- Make your enemies look like typical enemies, for example, red eyes and manic behaviors. They could be rabid animals that chase after the player or howling ghosts that jump out of walls to scare everyone.

The Final Boss

Remember when we spoke about first impressions? Creating one for your final boss is the most important; you want to strike fear in your player, so they know that when they come face to face with the final boss, they have a real challenge on their hands.

Who can ever forget Darth Vader's entrance to the *Star Wars* film *Rogue One*? This was one of the best entrances to an enemy in cinema. While this was a film, all fans can remember how dangerous and frightening he looked when he defeated the rebels in the corridor. That's the sort of impression you want to create for your boss, and make your player brace themselves. The beauty of this is that you can make this entrance at the start of the game or as a first and final reveal of the boss at the end of the game. If you chose to have the entrance at the beginning, then you want your player to know that who they're meeting will be what their game is leading to. In *Ratchet & Clank: Tools of Destruction*, the player meets the main boss, Emperor Tachyon, after the game's tutorial. While this wasn't a dramatic entrance, this was made humorous, and the game didn't take itself seriously, which fit the theme of the game series perfectly. But despite the jokes and quips, the player could tell that they would be facing off against Tachyon at the end of the game.

In some games, you may face off against the final boss numerous times so the player can learn the boss's move style and strategize for later in the game. *Star Wars Jedi: Fallen Order* will pit you against Trilla, a Sith Inquisitor, on multiple occasions in order for the player to put their skills to the test. While Trilla's health will never be reduced to zero during these fights, seeing her pop up can be frustrating. Not because it's another boss fight, but more because you weren't expecting her. The great thing about fighting the boss throughout the game helps give the player "history" with the boss. Alternatively, if you are wanting to keep the final boss battle till the end of the game, why not introduce smaller boss battles with other enemies? This can help practice the player's skills and build them up to the final battle. This can also help with player progression and building upon their journey through the game experience as well as introducing more of the story to them. If this is something you will want to incorporate, then think carefully about the designing of these boss battles. How will they impact the player? What benefit will they gain from facing them? How will you reward them for defeating these bosses?

One thing you want your player to have when approaching a boss fight is for your player to think about what they will achieve once they beat this boss. Without a good reason, then you will have no drive to keep fighting the boss and complete the story. If you are defeated by the boss on multiple occasions to win the game, you will become frustrated and want to keep trying, and so a grudge toward this boss begins. You also want to have a grudge against the boss if they have killed a favorite character or done something that simply fits the profile of a villain. Whatever your boss does, it needs to impact the gameplay and story and, at times, gives the player their goal for the game. Bowser steals the princess, so Mario goes to rescue her.

But don't always give the player all of the power; you want your enemies to look like they are winning or have the advantage. Make sure that even if the player chooses the easiest difficulty of the game, they will still take a hit. It might make the player think, "That wasn't much of a hit at all!", but give your enemies a cheap shot and deal some damage to your player. This makes it look like it's an even fight and will also encourage your player to hit back harder! to hit back at their enemies harder! The player isn't going to want to fight an enemy if they don't put up a challenge, even if the player is on the easiest difficulty, and the victory over them will feel hollow. No matter the difficulty setting, the player needs to feel that they are in danger when greeted by a group of enemies, and the player should feel like their encounter might be a struggle, or where will the fun be?

When we hear the words "Boss Battle," we immediately think of something or someone that has greater amount of health compared to other enemies you've faced, possibly larger in size, and something that will take skill and time to beat. But what about when it comes to making your own? I have seen many designers try to make a boss and create a battle scene around it, but it boiled down to just giving this enemy more health and not really thinking about the other important aspects of a boss battle. When designing one, there are lots of moving parts that need to be considered, such as the battle being fun, how does it flow with the story, and has the player learned enough to battle the boss? Here are a couple of methods you could think about when designing your own:

The player's moves – If your boss battle is at the end of the game, then you want to ensure that your player knows all of the necessary moves they need to defeat the boss. There should be no learning at this point, except for the way the boss fights.

A final weapon or ability – Allow the player to know that final special move that has been mentioned in the story and was being saved until they are ready to fight the boss, or grant them that fabled weapon to vanquish evil. You get the picture! You could give the player one final thing to learn for the battle, and they can practice it during combat.

Or use a combination of the two. I'm not suggesting that either of them is the correct method to use, but when it comes to your game, you can decide on what suits the idea better.

What about the appearance of your boss? The best way to design it is to think about the world you are playing in. In *Call of Duty: Modern Warfare 2*, you play as a soldier in Task Force 141, where the main antagonist was Shepherd, who was an Officer in the US Army. Quite fitting for the final boss to be someone in the Army. In *Ratchet & Clank: Rift Apart*, Dr Nefarious was the final boss, and it was fitting for a robot to have a gigantic robot suit to use to face off against the player. The boss needs to fit with the style and theme of the game you want to make. Here are a few other aspects to think about:

- What does the player gain from beating the boss? In most cases, it will mean victory in the story and beating the game; in others, it might mean the player has unlocked a weapon, ability, or character. But when it comes to the story, it might mean the character has gained something more than power or abilities. In *Star Wars Episode 5: The Empire Strikes Back*, Luke has learned that Darth Vader is his father and that he must continue his training to become a Jedi.

- What makes a final boss a true adversary for the player? As mentioned, we think of size, health, strength, etc., but you need the player to think they are in trouble before they even begin to think about the final boss or starting the encounter.

- What is your boss's motivation? All bosses have a reason for them being bad and a goal they want to reach. Careful consideration for their motives gives them more of a reason for just being "evil." Darth Vader wanted suppression and order to the galaxy. Whatever their goals and motives, they need to conflict with the main character's. This will lead the main character down their own path, which, of course, creates the story.

- What does the final boss represent to the protagonist? It could be that the boss is stopping world peace or love or the inner demons of the character. It could be that defeating the final boss would mean the protagonist is free to become who they are meant to be.

And that's it, you should know enough now to start to design the appearance of your enemy, its abilities, as well as the motivation it needs that will trigger your protagonist's story. But now we can start to pay attention to the smaller details of making your boss a formidable foe.

Attention to Detail

If there is an important thing to think about when designing anything in your game, it's paying close attention to detail. This also needs to be applied when designing your boss. As we mentioned before, size matters when it comes to making a final boss and giving the player a sense that they are going to struggle with the challenge. This section focuses on the thoughts of having a large enemy to defeat.

A top tip when it comes to making an enemy is thinking about the camera position. We've spoken about cameras in a previous chapter, but this is a great time to refer back to this. If you place your camera too high, then you lose sight of your character, and you struggle to see what moves they are making. If you place the camera too low, then the player struggles to see where the boss is and any incoming attacks.

In a previous chapter, thinking about elevation and being able to climb up walls or cliffs help give the player a chance to reach higher points of the boss for those extra-damage attacks. Keeping a boss fight all on solid ground can be bland and keep the battle repetitive. What happens if the boss comes down to the player's height? Fighting dragons in *Skyrim* is an excellent example of fighting an enemy in the sky and then on the ground. If the player deals enough damage to the dragon while they are in the air, the dragon will come to the ground and attack the player at close range. This gives the player a chance to deal extra damage in hand-to-hand combat where ranged attacks might deal less damage. But it also gives the player an even fight and stops them from feeling that they are at a disadvantage of only being able to travel on foot.

When you are fighting a larger boss, then you can have them deal large attacks. In *Avengers: Infinity War*, Thanos threw a moon at Iron Man, and Darth Vader threw bridges and large items at the player in *Star Wars Jedi: Fallen Order*. The more dramatic the attacks are from your boss, the more memorable they will be. You want your boss to have a lasting memory on your player, and provide them with a fight they will always remember. But also give some room for your player to strategize and understand your boss's attacks and moves. These are what we call patterns.

Patterns consist of enemy attacks and moves which are strung together to create predictable moves that the player can learn. In most cases, boss attacks might use a sequence such as this (we will call this Sequence 1):

- Charge up attack

- Attack

- Charge up attack

- Attack

- Cool down (which leaves the boss open to attacks from the player)

Over time, this sequence might become faster and challenges the player's reflexes and button pressing. If you have a large boss which moves around, they might use a sequence like this (we will call this Sequence 2):

- The boss chases the player around the map/arena.

- When in proximity, they swing/discharge their weapon or jump to make shock waves.

- The boss carries out Sequence 1.

- Repeats Sequence 2.

Movement sequences should be easy to remember, but feel free to change them around to avoid complete predictability of your boss. Still make sure that your player has something they can follow and remember.

Using sequences gives the player a chance for them to understand their boss and when they expose their vulnerable states. But the boss must be able to deal damage at any point during the sequences, which will, in turn, give the player something for them to avoid and prepare for. There is a chance that the player could avoid taking damage altogether, but this would make the battle too easy.

There are also times where the player has to sit back and avoid taking any damage. For the brave players, they might be able to deal damage to the boss while the boss is attacking the player, but there also needs to be times where the player has to do anything other than avoid being hit. These can be invulnerable attacks that stop the boss from taking any damage at the time.

Once the invulnerable attacks are finish, this might leave the boss in a vulnerable state to receive deadly attacks from the player. This might expose the boss's main weakness that the player can exploit. This should be the chance where the player can deal the most damage. These weak spots should be typically easy to spot on the boss, even if they aren't shown from the beginning. Your final boss might be a giant mech, and the only way to beat it is when the vents are exposed from overheating. These could be glowing bright red/orange to show the player where they need to deal their damage. When the player does attack, it should be during a state where the player can't be hit back, and they only have a few seconds to deal as much damage as possible. When the state is over, then make it clear that no more damage can be taken. Your boss might blow back the player to say: "You're done now, let's keep fighting!" and start the sequences all over again.

The final fight can only end one of two ways: the boss's defeat or the player's defeat. But this fight needs to be packed full of action to keep the fight going. If the player is injured, will you give them a chance to heal? This gives the player a chance to explore what tools they have around them to succeed. Giving the right abilities and power-ups in the world around them can provide that excitement that a boss battle needs.

Whatever you decide to make the final battle play out, there is always one thing that you need to do: let the player have the final strike. If this is given by a side character or anything but the player, then they lose that feeling of overcoming the boss and beating the game. Don't let that special moment go to someone else! Once the boss is dead, give the player a chance to put their controller down/set away from the keyboard and enjoy an animation/cutscene which shows the next step in the story. This is also the break the player deserves once they know they've beaten the game. The final part should feel like the ending of a movie, where the player can sit back and see how the story ends. Let the player savor the moment in their victory.

But what happens if the player fails to beat the boss? Ensure that you have a point where the player can respawn and carry on. For difficulty, having the player respawn and start the battle again is a great way to have them practice their moves and strategies and what works best to beat the boss. Also, never let the player jump right back into a boss fight until they are fully ready. There is nothing worse than losing a battle and jumping right back in without stocking up on ammo again, restoring health or armor, etc. Allow the player a chance to catch their breath before they jump back in again.

The Setting

The final thing to consider when making a boss fight is the setting. In some games, the setting can also be just as dangerous as the boss itself. Just as we've covered before, the environment and setting are important to get right as this can determine the move style of the boss and how they react to the world around them.

You may not have noticed it in previous games you have played, but boss fights tend to take place in a circular arena style. The great thing about this setting is that the camera will always be locked onto the boss, which means they will always be in view for the player. Just as we have covered in Chapter 5, having height and elevation to your level will help give different angles to fight at. This can help alternate a static playstyle and a dynamic playstyle (this means not having your player on the ground the whole time which can be quite boring!).

You need to think about how the boss will use the level to their advantage. Having the level break around you could give the boss a chance to throw things at you. This could also lead to other obstacles other than the boss to avoid, such as holes in the floor which lead to lava or cliff edges breaking which could lead to your death. This helps keep the level exciting but also challenging. The issue with this is that if the player keeps dying during the boss battle, the level will become bland and predictable if the player knows when and where the level will break. Alternatively, you could design the destruction of the level to be at random; this will help the battle feel fresh but not too predictable.

Designing your level with elements that can be destroyed can be the best way to show your dynamic flair. It also creates a unique experience for your player. In *Spider-Man* (PS4), the player needs to throw objects at Electro to incapacitate him before they can make their attacks. Rather than keeping it simple and punching your way through the fight, Insomniac gives the player a chance to use the world around the player as well as any abilities they have picked up to beat Electro. Using a combination of skills/moves helps keep things exciting.

What happens if you are battling in more than one place? When fighting Calamity Ganon in *The Legend of Zelda: Breath of the Wild*, Link fights the boss in Hyrule Castle, but the arena is flat and allows the player to circle around the boss to deal damage. However, in *Uncharted: The Lost Legacy*, Chloe is riding on top of a train and must move to the front to find the bomb and beat the boss. This includes a chance to jump from the train to vehicles such as cars and bikes before returning to the train. This is an excellent example of a dynamic playstyle and keeps the player on their toes on how to reach the final boss. While these are really cool to play, they require more work and closer attention to detail compared to arena-style levels.

Conclusion

So far within this chapter, we have covered the following:

1. What do you need to consider when designing an enemy?

2. What sort of enemies are there?

3. How to design a boss and its playstyle?

4. How will the level impact the final boss battle?

As Chapter 6 ends, we have covered some of the most important aspects to consider for the game's setting. We can now start to think about the three pillars that some of the greatest games have focused on: mechanics, combat, and multiplayer. While not all games make use of these pillars, a combination of all helps create something memorable.

CHAPTER 7

MCM (Mechanics, Combat, and Multiplayer)

Super Mario, Sonic, Space Invaders, Pong, Pokémon, Final Fantasy, Elder Scrolls, and *The Legend of Zelda* are just a handful of some of the greatest games ever made, and that was due to the attention of three crucial pillars when it comes to designing a video game: mechanics, combat, and multiplayer. While not all of the mentioned games include these pillars, at least one of them has been developed upon to create something timeless. During this chapter, we will be delving further into these pillars and how you can consider them when it comes to designing your game.

Mechanics

Ever seen a car drive with no wheels? Or a plane flying with no wings? Both rely on those things to work and become what they are supposed to be. And video games without mechanics are no exception. The meaning of mechanics in video games refers to objects that create gameplay when interacted with. The key to good mechanics is combining them with well-designed levels and enemies. Some mechanics can include

- Pushable items
- Levers and switches
- Moving platforms
- Wall running
- Grapple hooks

M. Killick, *The Way We Play*, https://doi.org/10.1007/978-1-4842-8789-7_7

Platforms are some of the most used mechanics in video games, especially within platformers (hence the name!). These can move left to right, up and down, crumble when stepped on, vanish, and then reappear. The possibilities are endless!

Another common mechanic used within games is doors. They are everywhere and can hide so much. Whether they are normally open or locked, there are unusual ways that the player can open them, either burst through them and shoot everything on the other side, slowly open them and peek round them if you are trying to be stealthy, breach and clear, or pick the lock. Once unlocked or opened, how would you like your doors to open? Up and down, side to side like an elevator, or with the traditional method of them swinging open. Different methods and doors are used in varied genres. Up and down would typically be seen in space stations or futuristic games and aliens bursting through doors to chase the player. Normal swinging doors could have enemies behind them which could be knocked or damaged when opened. While you can be creative with the way doors are opened, there are a few things you need to be careful with, such as the clipping of the player on the door. There will always be instances during the development stages where the player will walk through a door and the door clips the player, or the player will pass through the door without it opening. There are ways around this, such as not having any doors! While that sounds contradictory, some environments use buildings that use doors or look like they have been ripped off or damaged. Or in some cases, doors will never be opened, which prompts the player to find an alternative route. But you need to ensure that the player knows that they can't pass through them. *Star Wars Jedi: Fallen Order* does it perfectly when it comes to doors and pathways around the world. The player will encounter a door that might be locked, but once finding a new path and progressing further into the story, the player will be able to unlock the door from the other side, thus unlocking a "shortcut" for future exploration.

But what if you need more than a key to open a door or pass through something? Levers and switches are another wonderful way to open doors or even move cranes to move debris which is blocking your path. *Ratchet & Clank* games often use the Omniwrench to turn cranks that would move objects. While this is a good mechanic for the player to use, the designers try not to overuse it. There is nothing more stagnant than to use something multiple times at the same level. Be clever about the use of levers and switches and where to put them. If you want your game to feel natural, or realistic to some degree, having a lever in the middle of a room screams: video game. While that sounds silly, try to make this sort of mechanic fit in with the design and feel for your game. If you do decide to make these within your game, have a think about the following:

- Give a visual indication that the lever or crank has been pulled so the player knows it has been pulled or activated.

- Make it stand out! The last thing you want is your player to be stuck in a room and not knowing what they need to do next to progress. If you are teaching them how to use this mechanic early on in the game, make sure that they know what it looks like, so they remember to keep an eye out for them. Once familiar with them, it should be muscle memory on what to do next when approaching them.

Hazards

One of my favorite things about levels are the hazards the player needs to avoid. They might look and act like mechanics, but they often have a predictable pattern that is used to defeat the player. Some might be the following:

- Buzz saws

- Exploding barrels

- Lava pits

- Falling blocks/spikes

- Laser-sighted turrets

I've always admired the use of hazards in *Super Meat Boy* and the way that Edmund McMillen and Tommy Refenes used them in their game. Early on in the game, the player is introduced to buzz saws that are static and span on the spot. As the player began to learn that these were harmful, the buzz saws made another appearance and began to move side to side. These saws also began to move up and down sides of a wall and, eventually, spin around on giant sticks. Although these saws were used in unusual ways, they were always the same saw. Be clever about your assets and how they appear in your game!

When designing hazards, you want them to look dangerous and deadly while also getting them to fit in the world. For example, if you are making a first-person game set in the modern day, then you might want to have turrets that shoot the player. You might want to take inspiration from *Call of Duty* games. A safe way for the player to learn that something is dangerous is to have it attack the player! It's one thing to learn if a hazard is deadly, but it's another to learn from taking damage. But also take inspiration from dangerous items from the real world, such as lasers, fire, bombs/explosives, etc. No matter the design or the style of hazards, always ensure that you are using the correct colors and sounds to show real threat and danger.

When making hazards, there is one thing you never want to make: hazards that cause instant death. These can become tedious and boring after a while. It's better to let your player die from misadventure with a hazard than to kill them the first time. This allows the player to learn and understand their threats and what they can do to survive. The better way around this is to offer a difficulty setting for your game. As games are growing in size and content, designers now give the chance for players to choose their preferred experience. These are some typical difficulty settings found in games:

- Story mode – Lighter combat and gives the player a chance to explore the story.

- Light – For players who want to experience light combat and don't play many games.

- Moderate – For the average player who enjoys a balanced experience.

- Hard – Experienced players who enjoy a challenge. Skills will be tested.

- Very hard – For those that have played hard for their first playthrough and would like a greater challenge for their second run.

A difficult game will do whatever it can to punish the player while providing a memorable experience. However, a challenging game will require the player to use skill to overcome challenges and can feel more rewarding. But this is down to your opinion and the type of games you play! But there are some players who love difficulty and love to die in games – games such as *Demon's Souls, Elden Ring, Super Meat Boy, Cuphead, I Wanna Be the Guy: Gaiden, Bloodborne,* and many more. I have tutored many students who love difficult games and love the challenge, so I applaud you for completing those games!

How is your timing? Have you got good reactions? Well, you might need them to avoid that swinging blade or that fire that spits out of the ground! Having mechanics that are based on time is a fantastic way to test the player's reactions. They're also great for creating tension in your level and can require a proficient level of concentration. If you decide to use this method, make sure that the movement is simple: back and forth, up and down, left to right. If the movements are random, then this will be too difficult and almost unfair. You want your player to use skill with this mechanic, not luck. Being able to pass or cross over them must be tricky, but never impossible. Everything in your game must be achievable! If you want to give some hints about when to go, your character could say something to give the player a prompt to move. Again, make it a challenge, but not impossible!

But how does this look if we start to put everything we have covered so far into a first level? Feel free to follow this as a guide for your first level!

- Start your player in an open space to learn movement, walking and jumping.

- Introduce your first mechanic that the player can practice with. This should come early in the game to keep the player engaged and for them to learn.

- Once the first mechanic has been mastered, now add a second one in. This could be combined with the first mechanic.

- Now add in a hazard. The player has learned mechanics, and now they need to learn what might hurt them and what they will need to avoid in the game.

- Throw in some enemies! This should be a gradual build-up and let the player know who they might face off against.

- Mix the enemies and hazards together to make it interesting! Having mechanics and hazards working together can be a perfect recipe and can help with the designing of future levels.

How does that sound? It can be easy to learn the basics of your game from that first level, but how you populate it and design the world would be up to you!

Save Yourself!

Something that we will mention again later in this chapter is checkpoints. The perfect way for the player to take a breather and reflect on what they have just completed. Some games use campsites, beds, inns, and houses for the player to enter and rest. They might also be the perfect place to upgrade gear, regain health, or use acquired skill points.

The purpose for checkpoints is for the game to save progress of the player so far. Some earlier games would require the player to manually save the game from the menu or reach a safe zone. With more recent systems, games will now save automatically at checkpoints to save the player some time.

One piece of advice I can give when designing checkpoints is to not place them in a combat sequence. There is nothing worse than being spawn killed! Checkpoints can be useful if a player were to die in combat and they can spawn back in, but place the checkpoints somewhere within the combat where the player will be safe from being killed when respawned. *Halo: Combat Evolved* used this method carefully and had the game save a checkpoint once the player had killed a certain enemy. Once the game knew the player was safe, it would save their progress to allow them to continue their journey.

Some checkpoints might be visible or in the background of the game's system. If you want your checkpoint to be visible, make sure that it is clear that it is a target for the player to reach. Visible checkpoints can look "gamey" and might require a section in the tutorial to explain how and what they are. Making them invisible will not break the immersion for the player, but make it clear when the checkpoint has been reached to avoid the player having to manually save the game after they defeat an enemy. It can become awfully long-winded!

The Art of Combat

When you hear the word combat or violence, you could list many games you have played that include this. Some games are violent but show little or no blood, and there are some games that are extremely violent and do not hold back on the blood and gore. However, it is not as easy to think of a game, create a character, and give it a gun to shoot everything in the world. The designing of combat takes time and patience to ensure that it is designed with a purpose. Not everything has to involve shooting the other person!

However, there are many games out there that don't rely on violence or combat to complete them, such as *Bejeweled*, *Pong*, *Tetris*, and *Temple Run*. In these cases, violence is never the answer! There are plenty of other games where violence and combat are not needed. The age-old question when it comes to violence in video games is: Do violent video games make people violent? While I can't offer an answer to this question, (mainly as this subject sparks a huge debate among gamers), it is something to consider when designing combat in a video game. Violent video games require time and skill to complete design, but combat might be designed as part of the story rather than it being a core mechanic.

So why use combat in video games? The answers are easy:

- It creates an empowerment feeling for the player.

- A straightforward way for the player to be rewarded for their actions.

Ever faced an enemy and thought: "This is going to be a challenge, but I'm going to try it anyway!" Knowing that you have fought and defeated an enemy should give you a feeling that you have been able to overcome a challenge. This is crucial for the player, so they know that they have put their skills to the test and, more importantly, used their combat skills correctly and for fun. Also, providing rewards from defeated enemies is the perfect achievement for any player, whether it be health, ammo, currency, or abilities. Constant rewards for combat help entice the player to trigger a form of combat.

Style of Violence

But what sort of violence is there? We typically think of the bloody kind which leads to heads being ripped off and blood splattered over our screens, but there are five diverse types of violence we see within video games:

- Violence – Combat that will involve gore and blood.

- Fantasy violence – Scenes that involve human and nonhuman characters in a fantasy nature.

- Cartoon violence – Actions where cartoon-like characters are involved in violence may come out unharmed afterward.

- Comic violence – Slapstick violence that creates humor.

- Intense and graphic violence – Realistic violence and possible decapitation. Extreme gore, blood, and injury detail.

As mentioned about combat, the choice of violence must come with a purpose. Games such as *The Last of Us* use graphic violence to emphasize survival and the danger that the player faces. Most other zombie or post-apocalyptic theme games use graphic violence to add the element of fear and create atmosphere. This is understood, but the inclusion of any shooting, hitting, and killing could raise your PEGI rating when submitting it to a marketplace. A higher content rating could limit your chosen market and the audience you pitch or sell your game to.

Style of Combat

If you have decided on your type of violence you wish to design for your game, you now need to think back to how it will fit with the style of character and combat. In previous chapters, we have thought about how to design a character and their personality, and this is also the case when it comes to designing their combat.

Thinking about *The Last of Us* again, one of the main protagonists, Joel, is a father figure to Ellie and comes across as a strong and caring person. But during combat, he will do anything to protect those around him, even if that means demonstrating intense and graphic violence. But what about other well-known characters?

- Sackboy – Comic and bouncy

- Spider-Man – Nimble and fast

- Master Chief – Brutal and strong

- Soap MacTavish – Stealthy and good with weapons

Once you have designed your personality, now you need to think about how it fits into your chosen genre. What sort of gameplay experience do you want your players to feel? The choice of weapons will also come into play here as this will reflect the environment you have designed. Will you want your players to craft their own weapons in a survival game? Or will they start with a certain weapon? Or maybe even a signature weapon? From Master Swords to grapple hooks. Fire flowers to web shooters. Some of the most successful and well-known characters have had an iconic weapon that makes the gameplay and character memorable. The more original the idea for a weapon, the better!

Now as you have thought about which style of combat you want to use and relation to the genre/gameplay, we can now start to think about the designing of the combat itself. There are four main types of combat:

- Close range – Hand-to-hand combat, knives, grapples, etc.

- Medium range – Melee weapons and kicks.

- Long range – Combat that can be carried out from a distance using projectiles.

- Surrounding effects – These could be special abilities that affect the battlefield around you.

Once you have thought about the distance that the player will be when they meet their enemies, then you can decide which best suits your combat. Sackboy mainly uses close combat to defeat enemies, and Master Chief mainly uses a mixture of close, medium, and long ranges through the use of melee weapons and projectiles.

Chosen your style of combat? Good! Now we look at something called elevations. This is the understanding of giving the player a variety of combat. Using varied heights, you can deliver a variety of attacks the player can master. Using elevations can also be delivered horizontally and vertically. Some enemies use shields to protect them from close- and medium-ranged attacks, but they can only be defeated by attacking them from the air. Elevations consist of standing, low, high, and aerial. All give the player the advantage to mix up their gameplay experience.

Combat Controls

What about the buttons? While we have covered the use of controls and buttons in game design, now choosing which buttons carry out which move is crucial to create a balanced gameplay. Being able to also master timings when pressing a button is also one of the major keys to combat. When a player presses a button, the character should perform the attack in the same moment. While some games might use buildup animations to create suspense and power up, these can become a drag and throw the player off their experience. Furthermore, a player could build up an attack which could miss (which can happen!), but the constant watching of an animation can make the gameplay feel like a drag and cause frustration. On the other hand, the use of these animations makes wielding weapons such as a large sword to deal vast amounts of damage look cool! It can help make the gameplay look more dynamic and satisfying. However, hitting moves and buttons in quick succession will lead to smoother gameplay, but also allows games to fall into the category of "button mashers." These games get their name from their combat experience. A player might need to press multiple buttons that play out a sequence of moves but with no strategy behind it and hope that they land a hit on their enemies. Games such as *For Honor* or *Tekken* require the player to think about the buttons they are pressing. In some cases, pressing buttons in a certain sequence could lead to a "chain."

A chain is a sequence of attacks that can lead one after another. By carrying out these attacks in quick succession (and successfully!), these can lead to the player dealing copious amounts of damage. Ever seen in a boss fight when you land a chain of attacks, and the boss moves away and begins their attacks? A few things happen here to avoid the boss fight being too easy:

- As the player makes their attacks, each of the moves sees the character lunging forward to keep the enemy within their combat range.

- The enemy will play an animation that parries the player to allow their attack chain to begin. This breaks up the combat to avoid the player from dealing all the damage.

- The enemy might be recharging, regaining health, or incapacitated which allows the player to begin their combat chain again.

But what happens when you actually land that perfect hit? How will your enemy react? When landing a hit, you should be hitting three crucial senses:

- Sound

- Sight – Animations and camera

- Touch – Vibrations

If you want your fight to feel like a real fight, you need to think about what you would see if you were to swing that sword or fire that shot. When a player lands a hit on an enemy, there should be a stagger animation or a reaction to show that the enemy has taken a hit. The camera also needs to be locked onto the player so they can see the world around them. In third-person games, the camera might pan up to show more of the battlefield and so the player can get a better look at their surroundings. But you can also use the camera to be dramatic with final blows or those special moves. In the *Batman Arkham* series, the camera cuts in close and slows down time to demonstrate the player has defeated the final enemy in a wave. In *Marvel's Avengers*, when landing the final blow on larger enemies, the camera cuts to each of the Avengers to show their final fights before the camera returns to the player. At the same time, the player needs to hear that they landed the hit. This could be from a bang to an Oof! When fighting the daughters of Lady Dimitrescu in *Resident Evil Village*, each of them screams when they take damage.

The last thing they should feel is some feedback through vibrations in a controller (this mainly applies to console games due to vibration limitation on a PC). By considering these senses, you can create an immersive experience for your player.

In some third-person games, the player is given the chance to lock the camera onto their chosen enemy. This can be greatly beneficial as all animations and combat will be locked toward one target. The player can either take out their enemies one by one using the camera, or they can eyeball it and attack everyone at once!

What about when your fight is coming to its end? How will you want the player to finish off their enemy? Of course, you could have them hit their enemy, and they fall down and collect the rewards, but what if you wanted to land that dramatic final punch? This is where your new friend quick time events (QTE) come into play. This is a list of buttons pressed in succession that prompted on the screen. Ever seen in combat where a button might appear to land an attack? What you experienced was a QTE. These can be particularly useful if you want to create a strong sequence for your combat. For example:

- The beginning – The player meets their enemy and engages in combat. The camera might pan around the battlefield to assist the player with any items they might need or places to cover before focusing on the enemy itself and then back to the player to begin the fight.

- The middle – The player is fully engaged with the enemy and carrying out chains and their combat sequence. They have the chance to practice their combat skills and how they want to take on their enemy.

- The end – The player engages in a QTE to finish the battle. The enemy might have little health, and the QTE is triggered to finish them off. This allows the player to feel like they have mastered the battle and brings it to an awesome and choreographed close.

While this was a suggestion for how they can be implemented into a combat sequence, be wise when using them if you do. Have a think about the following when designing QTEs:

- QTEs should only be used to create some of the most awesome and pivotal moments in your game. QTEs are about assisting the player to create badass moments, so you'll need to think: "Is this the right time to use it?" But you also need to consider what you are giving a QTE for; can it be done by the player themselves?

- Give the player enough time (but not too much!) to recognize the button on the screen for them to press it. Some games use a circle indicator getting smaller around the button to show how much time they have to press it

- When the button prompt on the screen appears, make sure that it always appears in the same place. Consistency is key!

- There will be times where the player misses their timing or presses the wrong button, so make sure that they get another chance at pressing it. If your QTE is made up of three buttons and the player fails to press the final button, restart the QTE but avoid killing the player for a simple mistake. It can be unfair if the player is killed for making a simple mistake, but it also gives them the chance to learn from this. Alternatively, you could kill the player for failing a QTE if the player is on a higher difficulty level. Then you can decide how easy you want your gameplay to be!

Forms of Combat

Now as we have the basics covered, we can look at the different forms of combat. These are defined into melee, stealth, and grapples.

Melee

The art of hand-to-hand combat and where melee weapons can make a distinctive feature. All first- and third-person games should have an element of melee combat if combat is present in the designing of the game. Think of all of the *Call of Duty* games; being able to swing your knife is considered as melee combat!

Being able to swing punches should deal some good damage, but finding weapons and items in the world should give an edge when in combat. Even in combat, make it easy for the player to pick up and drop weapons. Whether weapons break or run out of use during combat, the player should always be able to resort to their fists. When designing weapons, you need to think about their attributes such as speed, range, and damage. In *The Last of Us* series, some melee weapons have a certain amount of uses before they break. But they can also be upgraded to deal extra damage and last longer in combat. If weapons have been upgraded, make it clear that this is the case in a weapons menu and with a visual appearance. Having an upgraded weapon which shows the player's reward can make them feel empowered and make them want to begin their next fight. But what about special effects? Will your weapons have special effects that glow or spit fire or poison when used? Will your enemies disintegrate when hit or run away while on fire? Adding these effects makes using the weapon all the more satisfying.

Stealth

The *Assassin's Creed* games are built off this combat and wouldn't be where they are today without it. Stealth attacks are quick which are used to kill or disable an enemy without alerting others around them. While most are used in a crouch or hidden position, a QTE can be used here to give the player the chance to deliver an awesome hidden kill. This method should only be used under certain circumstances such as being hidden, in the shadows or in a certain place in the game. Otherwise, the player could defeat all enemies using this method rather than engaging in your well-designed combat. If you have awesome looking stealth kill animations and they are used all the time, things will become stale. Let the player experiment with their choice of combat.

Grapples

Ever hung over the edge of a cliff and an enemy is standing over you? We've all had that opportunity where we pulled an enemy off a cliff and thrown them to their doom. These are similar to stealth kills, but they require interaction with the enemy and can only be activated under specific circumstances. Some third-person games will require the player to engage in hand-to-hand combat, where they could be grabbed by the enemy, which will require the player to free themselves. A clever use of a QTE could help release themselves from the grapple and then finish off their enemy. Make getting out of your enemy's grasp easy so the combat doesn't feel one-sided. There is nothing worse than to be caught by an enemy and then killed immediately. Where is the fun in that?

Top Tip   While we play games, we ultimately want to be successful in their completion and gaining all the rewards and defeating the final boss. But when battling and fighting enemies, the player will need to miss a few hits. Ever seen a boxing match where every punch has landed successfully? Probably not. But letting the player miss their shot or landing their hits will only make them practice more. The more battles they face, the more hits they miss, and this will only make them more skilled as a player.

Always Moving

No combat has ever involved standing still. Boxing requires you to move around your opponent. Fencing requires the players to move forward and strike their opponents. Combat in video games is also the same. If you can avoid being hit during combat, then you are doing something right. The goal is not to get killed, so if that means dodging and moving out of the way from incoming attacks, then that's the case!

Most third-person games give the player a chance to dodge or roll out of the way for an incoming attack or something being thrown at them. When doing this, it should be easy to use and do, such as clicking a button or moving a stick to get the player out of the way. But there should be a moment after the dodge or roll has happened for the player to get back on their feet and carry on. When moving out of the way of an attack, you need to ensure that it has been designed and animated to avoid it. What's the point of having a dodge and not dodging anything when used? Make sure the player clears out of a blast radius or wide-range attacks, so they know their time and moves were effective.

Dodges and rolls can also be used to get the player out of tight corners and make them look awesome while doing it. If there is a door coming down or a spiked wheel heading straight for them, they can use their dodge or roll to avoid this. Getting past hazards in this way is also great practice for the player, and so they remember to use this ability during combat.

Nothing can beat an old-fashioned jump. Something so graceful but can also be a method to defeating your enemies. The most famous bouncer, Mario, uses this method for most of the enemies he faces. Of course, bouncing on a Goomba was the first thing the player could do when they played the first *Super Mario Bros*, and the player quickly learned that this was how you defeat any enemies. If a player should jump on an enemy to defeat them (this will depend on if you want your enemies defeated in this way), then there should be some positive recoil for the player, such as a second bounce which elevates them higher than a standard bounce. The player could use this to chain a bounce and defeat multiple enemies in quick succession. Having a reward for chain-killing enemies will encourage the player to do it again!

In *Ratchet & Clank: Rift Apart*, the designers added the option to dash. This can be used to move around the map quicker if the player didn't want to run everywhere, but its primary use was to avoid enemy fire. But this could also be used to dash into objects that could be broken. Having a dash in your game can be used to defend the player but can also be used as a form of attack. The player could dash toward an enemy which could cause them to stagger before dealing a powerful attack. Be clever about little abilities with this and think about how the player could use them to their advantage. This ability could also be upgraded in your game to allow faster and harder hitting dashes. It's up to you!

Blocking Your Enemies

Now you know how to design your character to attack their enemies, you now need to think about how they are going to block their attacks. Again, just like sports, every player needs to know how to avoid and block incoming attacks and defend themselves.

Blocking can be found mainly in action games which allow the player to defend themselves from an attack with just a press of a button. A block should be simple and no issues, which is why using one button is perfect for it. Whether you are blocking an incoming sword, punch, arrow, or lightsaber, it should be easy to use.

Some games allow the player to pick up shields during combat to even out a fight, but these shields might only be able to take a certain amount of damage before they break. Using breakable shields can be a clever technique to use if you want your player to take a breather during a battle. But shields can also have more than one purpose. Here are a few more suggestions for the use of shields:

- Smash through enemies or knock them back

- Throw a shield at enemies or targets

- Ride the shield down slopes

- Used as part of the level design and smash through to different areas

- Break through objects

Similar to giving a character a shield, armor is also a fantastic way to help a player defend themselves from foes. It is also a perfect opportunity to add customization into your game if this is something you are considering. Customization appears in all manner of games, but the changing of armor might appear more in mythical or fantasy games. But don't be mistaken by the appearance of armor, it also needs to be of benefit to your player. If a player ventures on a daring mission to retrieve some awesome looking armor, it needs to be of benefit to them and the gameplay. Make the reward worth their while! Armor is typically broken into different body sections, gauntlets, torso, legs, boots, and helmet. A player might start off with using weaker protection such as leather, before exploring the world and missions to gain upgraded armor. But give them a noticeable visual upgrade. You want them to look and feel awesome while wearing their rewards!

Health and Lives

The final thing to think about when it comes to combat is health. What is the point of engaging in combat but not being able to reduce an enemy's health to zero? Or even have the chance to die from engaging in combat? To ensure that everything that we have covered for combat matters, we need to think about health and lives.

Health is typically displayed either by colors or numbers. Colors can be clean and easy to determine if 70–100% health is green, 40–70% is amber, and 0–40% is red. Numbers can also be easy to read, but it's difficult to be creative with it. You also need to ensure that you use a clear font when displaying text on your screen. A health bar doesn't take up much room on your screen, and this can be designed to match your player. For example, *Halo* uses an energy shield which will reduce if enough damage is taken. It is still a health bar under the surface, but it's been designed to look like it's part of the Master Chief's helmet and part of his HUD (heads-up display).

Some games use health but never display a health bar. In most *Call of Duty* games, the loss of health is displayed through blood appearing on the screen. The more blood seen, the less health the player has. But this health can be regenerated over time. If you choose to use this method, make sure that it is dramatic and effective. You can slow down time while the player is regaining health, or a heartbeat and heavy breathing could be heard. Whatever you decide to do, make sure that the player knows that they are close to death, and they need to take cover!

When thinking about the amount of health a player should have, you will need to think about how much taking a hit from an enemy will cost. For example, if your player started with 10 hit points, and could only take 10 hits before they died, then the enemies will need to reduce 1HP for every hit they land. If health can be upgraded, then you will need to decide how much larger and more difficult enemies will take from the player's health when they land a hit.

If the player dies, will they lose a life? Or will they just continue from their most recent checkpoint? Lives are becoming an outdated approach to health, but you might see more of them in arcade and platformer style games. As games now take hours to complete, the need for lives seems useless. But during the times of arcades, lives were the best way for players to sink their money into machines to play again. Additional lives became an effective way for players to continue playing a game, but the use of lives itself was soon running its course. Players began to respawn from reloading checkpoints instead of worrying about the number of lives they had when games moved to home consoles. Now death was never a worry!

Designers soon clocked onto this and removed the life system from games and gave the players a chance to respawn from checkpoints or save points. The player could do this as many times as they liked until they completed their mission.

However, if you do decide that lives will be best suited to your game idea, then here are a few things to consider when implementing them:

- Make it clear that the player has lives and demonstrate that lives can be lost. The last thing you want is for your player to move through the game thinking they are invincible.

- Lives need to be clearly shown on the HUD, or health needs to be accessible for the player to see during gameplay.

- Keep death quick. If a player has three lives and there is a death animation playing, they will quickly get bored of watching the same animation for every life they lose. You could have a final animation displayed once the player has lost all their lives to show they really are dead.

- Make it clear that the player can gain more lives through the game.

- If they get lives back, make sure they want to continue with playing and not stop once they die completely. You want them to keep on playing!

If you lose a player, you may not get them back. Always give them a reason to keep going. If you can tease them for what they missed out on from dying, it might just keep them playing!

Multiplayer

Multiplayer, the mode that has evolved more than anything over the years. Once from crowding around an arcade machine to now playing with 30+ people over the Internet. One of the earliest multiplayer games I remember playing was *Halo: Combat Evolved* with my dad for the first Xbox. Being able to work together and fight the Covenant never felt so sweet. But as I got older and consoles became more advanced, I found myself starting to play online with my friends on *Call of Duty*, *Grand Theft Auto*, and *Overwatch*. The social era of games was starting to take hold.

But what sort of multiplayer modes are there?

- Head to head – Better known as couch play, this would bring players together in the same room to play the same game, whether this was to battle against each other or to work together toward the same objective. This would require using the same console and more than one controller.

- Network – More than just for shopping and social media, the Internet was the perfect way to connect gamers to play together. Some gamers might bring their PCs together and connect them via an Ethernet cable to play the same game. Gamers might host LAN parties where this would happen.

- Client-server LAN – Being able to play against or work with multiple players online changed the way we play games. This opened the door for large-scale maps where players would fight against each other for a common objective. Games such as *Fortnite* and *PUBG* changed the way client-server games were made and brought in the golden age of battle royale games.

If you decide that multiplayer is going to be an option for your game, then you need to decide which sort of multiplayer you wish to use:

- Competitive – Players have the same objective and must battle against each other to achieve the goal.

- Cooperative – Players must work together to achieve the same goal.

- Conjugate – Where players share the same map but will have different objectives. *Grand Theft Auto* and *World of Warcraft* use this method and bring thousands of players together with their own goals and missions.

But what about game modes? You might be able to play online, but what sort of modes will you offer if you chose to have a multiplayer mode? There are plenty to choose from, and you might have played some of these during your time:

- Survival – Staying alive! Players must stay alive while trying to achieve a goal. Normally, the goal is straightforward and will give the game more of an emphasis on the mode of survival.

- Creation – Creating and building worlds that can be visited by other players. *Minecraft* is the king for this and has a large following for players to build cities and towns and ultimately build an extension of their lives in a virtual world.

- Free for all – Every man for themselves and fights to the death. Most kills wins, nice and simple!

- Team DeathMatch – Players are put into teams to achieve a common goal. Teams may either be at random or decided based on parties of friends playing together.

- Racing/driving – Your typical race against the other players to achieve a particular goal, such as winning the race or time trials. *Mario Kart* is the perfect racing game, but has the potential to ruin relationships due to power-ups and the evil blue shell!

- Capture the flag – Team based where one person must collect a flag or objective and deliver it to a designated area. The supporting team will protect the carrier from dropping the flag and allowing the opposing team from picking it up and winning.

- King of the hill – Teams need to defend a designated area from their opponents for a certain period of time.

While these are different modes that you might have played or fancy adding into your game, there are a range of activities that can be achieved within these modes or just by playing the game. The beauty of online games is the social aspect; being able to speak to friends and go on missions together can help make an online game thrive, and designers capitalize on that. Why make a game online if you can't play with your friends? Most online games have a text or voice chat system that players can use to speak to their friends or other players. Some gamers like to use Discord, but some prefer to use the chat that appears in-game.

Player Customization

What players love about any game is being able to be someone they wish they were. The key to achieving this is through character customization. Players love it! I also love it! The level of player customization can begin from a template character from the start of a game to the player being able to choose sex, eye and hair color, body shape, tattoos, facial features, and more. Once the player progresses further in the game, they are given the chance to purchase clothing, weapons, armor, vehicles, and more. All of which can be customized to alter the player's appearance or playstyle. Some items can be won through minigames or sometimes through microtransactions or in-game currency. Everyone wants to look the best, so make sure that you design some awesome gear for your player to wear and unlock!

Player Interactions

On a more serious note, the world of online gaming can be a tricky one. While there are systems out there to support it, griefing other players can happen. This is when another player might harass or try to cause harm to another player. While some reading this might think that it might be part of the game, treating others fairly online is so crucial for everyone to have fun. While you might not know the person you are playing with, you need to treat them with the same respect you would expect to be treated with. Designers will implement policies for players and make it clear that there is a zero-tolerance policy of bullying or harassment. Everyone is here to have fun!

Multiple Worlds

Multiple worlds (a little bit like alternate realities!) are perfect for those players that wish to play with either themselves or just their friends. I find that playing with other random players can be a bit much when I want to chat with my friend, so we hop into our own server just to explore and chat. Sometimes when you want your own time complete missions and play your own way, you may not want other players try to kill you, and you can take the game at your own pace. Some servers or separate maps can offer setting rules such as no friendly fire or a passive mode where no weapons can be used. Think about how your game might benefit from having these settings and what might be best for it.

Something that I like to do a lot with my friends, are raids – the perfect way to assemble your friends and fireteams to take down a boss and reap the rewards. In my case, I like to do raids in *Pokémon Go* (yes, people still play that game!), and I get to meet up with friends (the social aspect coming in again!) and battle it out to catch the latest legendary. In MMOs (massively multiplayer online), friends would team up to bear difficult game scenarios, such as a difficult boss, storm buildings, or to take part in an in-game event to earn exclusive rewards. The key to working in a team is communication. Each player might bring their own set of skills or a class that works effectively against the boss or in collaboration with another player. The reason for their popularity? Being able to feel awesome. Marching into battle with your comrades and protecting them from enemy fire can be an empowering feeling. So, designing scenarios like this can be effective and challenging. You want your players to use creative thinking to overcome this challenge you have designed. But make sure that once the raid has been completed, everyone can reap the rewards and provide effective rewards based on a player's performance.

We spoke about griefing before, but make sure that there is no way that players can spawn camp. There is nothing worse than being killed in the same moment you spawn into a new game. This is unfair for players and provides an unfair advantage to those carrying out the killing. Some games have implemented an idle phase which will kick the player out of a game if they are idle for too long. *Grand Theft Auto 5 Online* removes a player from the online game if they are idle for 15 minutes. Don't be that player!

Sharing Rewards

Thinking about the social aspect of a game again, having a space where players can share rewards and show off trophies is a neat thing to have. *Pokémon Shining Pearl* and

Brilliant Diamond reinvented their original underground system where players could meet and visit their caves. They could show off trophies and rewards they have achieved from the main storyline and from treasures in the underground. *Animal Crossing*'s whole social aspect thrives off of this and allows players to visit other towns and villages to see their designs. Creating a world where the player could see themselves is an excellent social feature to incorporate.

As a summary, let's weigh up the pros and cons about including a multiplayer option into your game's design.

Pros

- Can bring and create communities within games. *Pokémon Go* has amassed a global community since its release in 2016 and this has led to many global in-person events for players to meet and play together. This has been down to the ability to play with others online as part of raids, trades, and battles.

- Being able to play cooperatively and competitively, has seen the rise in esports. These include packed-out stadiums where thousands of fans of teams and games come together to watch famous and talented teams compete for prizes. This can have a knock-on effect and help raise sales and awareness for games if fans see their favorite team playing a game competitively.

- Future content for a game can help expand the overall game but also offer a chance for new players to join. Online games such as *Destiny*, *Pokémon Sword and Shield*, *World of Warcraft*, and *League of Legends* see new online updates available for their players to keep them entertained long after the game's release. Remember when we spoke about making sure the player feels they get the most for their money? Well, expansion packs are certainly a way of doing this! Whether this is through levels and missions, characters, or raid battles, there is something for new and old players alike. Just be sure that if this is something that you would consider in the future for a game of your own or a game you are part of, the new content has a real place within your game. There is nothing worse than to create a new expansion and slap a £60 price tag which was the same price as the base game. Your players would not be happy!

Cons

- As mentioned before, playing games online can lead to a host of players being exposed to griefing and bullying. While this is something that companies take with great care and attention, there will always be players out there that fall victim to harassment online. There are, however, programs out there such as the Xbox Ambassadors Program that support equality and diversity in online games and encourage players to be fair to one another and create a positive space for players to play. (This last comment could also be seen as a positive too!)

- Where there are thousands of players, there will be a few that hack or cheat at your game. Some first-person shooters such as *Call of Duty* have been renowned for players cheating and using aim assist bots online. Companies are constantly working hard to squash cheating and develop anti-cheat methods to make their space a fair place to players.

- We mentioned earlier in the book about testing and providing early access to a game for players to help give them a feel before they commit to buying. If there is something more important to receive positive feedback from players, it is to get it from the press. With online modes typically open to the press and public prior to a release, the press will be the ones that review the game and provide honest feedback to those thinking about getting a copy. If the press fails to like it, then there is a likelihood that players will avoid purchasing a game entirely.

- Pricing was mentioned in the pros, but this can be a difficult discussion when it comes to charging your players for any extra online features. There are your typical in-game currency expansions that the player can use to purchase new items in a game, or there are expansions where the player must pay the same price for extra content which is the same price they paid for the original game.

Players can get iffy about this and sometimes wait for the price to come down in future sales, or they simply cannot afford it. Other games however, such as *Overwatch, Marvel's Avengers,* and *Grand Theft Auto V,* give free content updates to players in the form of weapons, characters, missions, and vehicles. This might lead developers to show road maps of their game to show when future updates will be release and what upcoming content the players can expect,

In the end, it will be your or your team's choice whether online features will make an appearance in your project. But just be sure that whatever you create, it will be a safe space for players to come together, but, more importantly, what the purpose of it would be.

Conclusion

So far within this chapter, we have covered the following:

1.   What are mechanics and how are they used/designed with games?

2.   What is multiplayer and what sort of modes can you design?

3.   How is combat designed and what do you need to consider?

4.   What are the benefits and drawbacks to having a multiplayer option within your game?

For your final practical tutorial, you will now be shown how to create a 2D platformer project within Unity. Not only will this give you the chance to explore the software further, this will also give you the chance to use this demo for the foundations of a game you could make in the future. This will be a step-by-step guide on how you can set your project up and begin to explore this method of play.

CHAPTER 8

2D Platformer Tutorial

For this chapter, you will now be shown how you can create the basics of a 2D platformer within Unity which can be used as the foundations for a future project or your first game. To set this project up, you will need to follow a similar process to the 3D first-person project from earlier in this book.

Set Up

If you haven't done so already, you will need to download Unity Hub which is the home for all updates, your projects, and installations of Unity. You can find this download from the Unity website.

Once downloaded and installed, you will need to create a free Unity account to start making projects. This will also allow you to sync any projects if you log in to a different machine in the future. It will also provide you with a free license to create games on your machine. If you ever create any games commercially, then you will need a professional license which you can purchase through Unity. Once set up, you will need to click the Install Editor button and select the version of Unity you would like to use. You can see this in Figure 8-1. I would recommend using the version that is recommended by Unity as this will be the most stable and up-to-date version at the time.

© Michael Killick 2022
M. Killick, *The Way We Play*, https://doi.org/10.1007/978-1-4842-8789-7_8

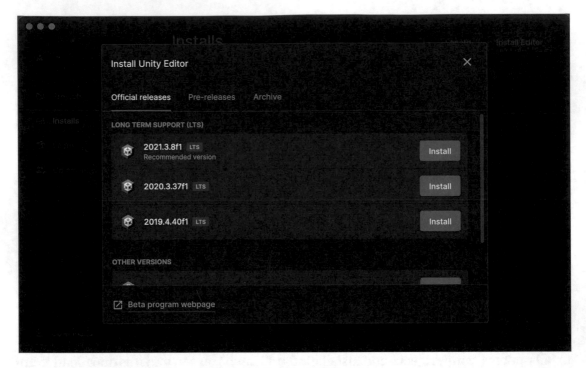

Figure 8-1. *Unity Hub and Unity software versions*

2021.3.8f is my recommended version to use, but do ensure that you select which one has been recommended by Unity to use for this tutorial. Once chosen, you will need to select some modules which will support Unity. As I am running a Mac, in the tutorial, you can see that it has been selected for me to have Visual Studio installed as well. This might not appear for you if you have already got Visual Studio installed on your machine. If you decide to use another code editor, then you can untick Visual Studio to be added. You will need to scroll through the list and choose either Mac Build Support or Windows Build Support, depending on the machine you are using. You are now ready to begin the install!

Once the software has been installed, you can now create a new project. Click the blue button which says New Project. On the left-hand side, choose Core. Then select 2D and give the project a name, such as "Platformer Test Build." You can see this in Figure 8-2. When you are ready, click Create Project and wait for Unity to open!

Figure 8-2. *Unity Hub with the selection of templates*

Step 1

We're going to begin with a simple Sprite made within Unity. Right-click in the Project window and select Create ➤ Sprite ➤ Circle. Make sure to name your sprite as "Player" so your assets can be organized appropriately. You can see this method in Figure 8-3.

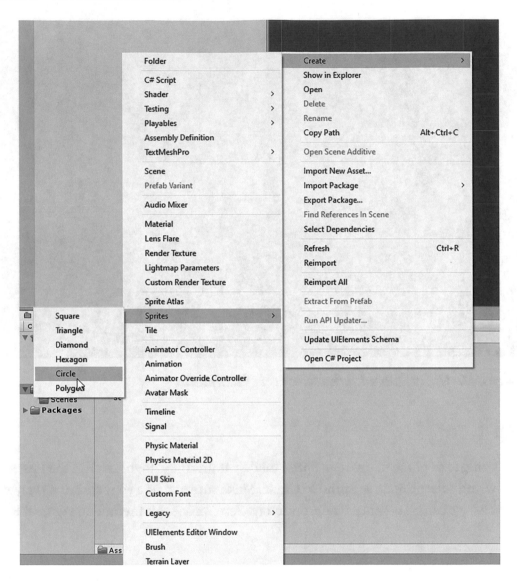

Figure 8-3.   *Creating a Circle object in the Asset viewer*

Drag and drop the Player sprite into your Hierarchy window. This will place the Sprite in the Scene at the coordinates 0, 0, 0 and turn this into a Player object.

Step 2

Now select the Player object that you have just created and, in the Inspector, click Add Component. Search for "playerScript," click New Script, and click Create and Add. This will not only create the script in our Project, but it will automatically add it to our Player object. You can see this in Figure 8-4.

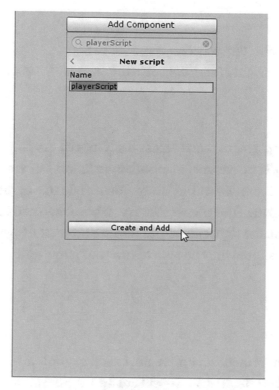

Figure 8-4. *Creating a new playerScript script*

Double-click the Script in the Inspector which will then open the script in your chosen code editor.

Step 3

Let's start by having our Player move from side to side. Add the following script into your chosen code editor:

```
public class playerScript : MonoBehaviour
{
    public float speed;

    void Start()
    {
```

```
    }

    void Update
    {
        float h = Input.GetAxisRaw("Horizontal");
        transform.Translate(new Vector3(h * speed * Time.deltaTime, 0, 0));
    }
}
```

This will allow our player to move across the X axis so the player can move left and right. Using Time.deltaTime ensures a smooth translation. Once completed, be sure to save the script so it can compile within Unity. You can do this by either pressing Ctrl+S or Command+S or clicking File ➤ Save. When you have returned to Unity, you need to look at the Inspector on the right side of the screen and set the Speed float to something greater than zero. You should now be able to run your game and see the player move from left to right!

Step 4

Now as we have our movement set up, we now need to apply an environment for our player to walk around on. To do this, we will create a simple tilemap that the player will be able to walk on and jump on. Start by adding a tilemap into your scene. You can see this in Figure 8-5.

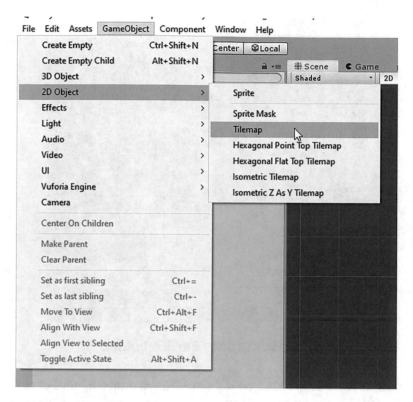

Figure 8-5. *Selecting the Tilemap from the 2D Object menu*

Next, open the Tile Palette as shown in Figure 8-6.

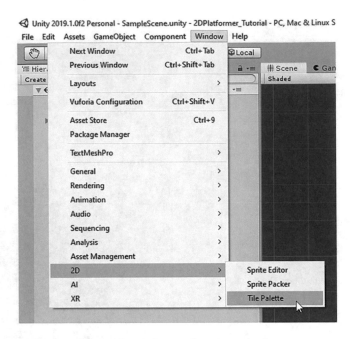

Figure 8-6. *Opening the Tile Palette from the 2D window*

Click **Create New Palette**, name your Palette "Environment," and click Create. Save this in the Assets folder of your Unity project, as shown in Figure 8-7 (It will open your file browser window by default). This will appear when you try to save the Environment.

Figure 8-7. *Tile Palette and creating the Environment palette*

Create a new square and call it Ground. (This is the same method we took to create the Circle which is now our player! You can see this in Figure 8-8.) Drag this onto your Tile Palette in the window (this should still be open from when you created your Environment) and save the file as "groundTile" in your Assets folder.

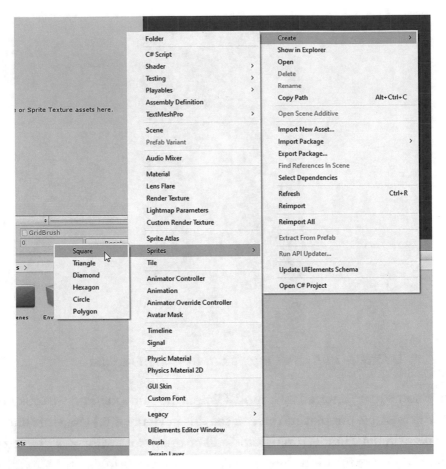

Figure 8-8. *Creating a Square object in the Asset viewer*

Making sure that you have the Brush tool selected in the Tile Palette window (you can see this button third from the left at the top of Figure 8-9), click the white square in the window, and then click and drag in empty to create your platforms.

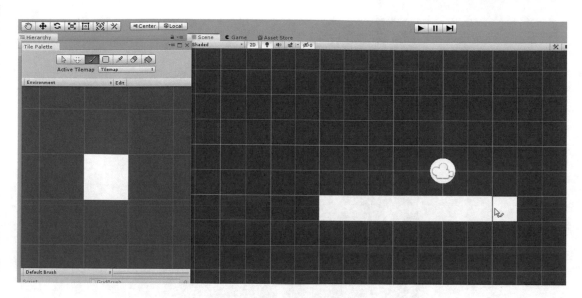

Figure 8-9. *Creating the ground using the Tile Palette*

Step 5

For your final step to making the environment, you need to allow the tilemap to collide with the player. Make sure that you select the Tilemap from the Hierarchy as shown in Figure 8-10.

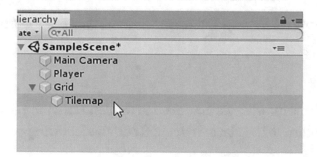

Figure 8-10. *Selecting the Tilemap object from the Hierarchy*

You now need to add a Tilemap Collider 2D from the Inspector as shown in Figure 8-11.

Figure 8-11. *Adding a Tilemap Collider 2D component in the Inspector*

Step 6

For the final part of this tutorial, we now need to implement a jump feature for our player. To do this, return to the playerScript and add the following code highlighted in **Bold**:

```
public class playerScript : MonoBehaviour
{
    public float speed, jumpForce;
    public Rigidbody2D rb;

    void Start()
    {
```

```
        rb = GetComponent<Rigidbody2D>();
    }

    void Update
    {
        float h = Input.GetAxisRaw("Horizontal");
        transform.Translate(new Vector3(h * speed * Time.deltaTime, 0, 0));

        if (Input.GetButtonDown("Jump"))
        {
            rb.AddForce(new Vector2(0, jumpForce), ForceMode2D.Impulse);
        }

    }
}
```

To get a better understanding of the code we have just added, *rb* references our RigidBody2D, and *AddForce* will add a force to any specified direction. We create a Vector2 (X and Y coordinates) just for this statement by writing *new Vector2*. We leave X as 0, and apply our jumpForce to the Y axis. The last element is identifying the application mode. *ForceMode2D.Impulse* will apply the force as a singular burst at that moment.

You can now save your script and return to Unity. You now need to add a Rigidbody2D and Collider to our object. This can be done in the Inspector with the Player selected. Click Add Component and search for Rigidbody2D and Collider within the list of components. You will need to select the most appropriate shape for your collider. However, in our case as we are using a circle as our character, you will need to use the Circle Collider.

Step 7

For some of the final steps, we need to create a Ground Check for the player to avoid falling through the ground. While testing your gameplay, you might have noticed that you can jump continuously. This is due to Unity not knowing whether we are allowed to jump or if we are on the ground. This is a mechanic that would fit into games such as *Flappy Bird*, but as we are making a platformer, we will need to keep it to a single jump.

We need to create an Empty Game Object that will serve as our reference when checking if we have touched the ground. We could use a collision check; however, this would enable our player to wall jump or jump when touching the ceiling as well. By using a Ground Check, we can limit it so jumping is only enabled when the player touches the floor. You can see this in Figure 8-12.

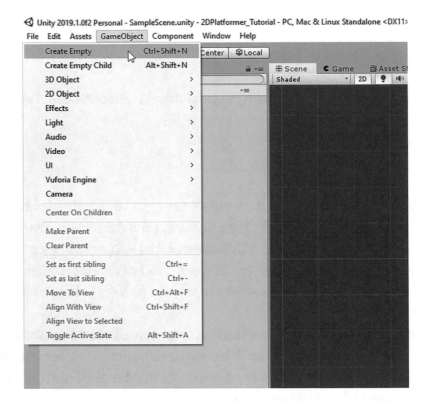

Figure 8-12. *Creating an empty object from the GameObject menu*

With your new object created, give it the name "Ground Check" and make it a child of the Player object by dragging it on top of it in the Hierarchy.

Step 8

We now need to place this new object under our Player in the Scene, so it intersects with the floor whenever we are on the ground. Select the Ground Check object and press the W key to use the Move tool. Drag the object just below the Player. You can use Figure 8-13 as a reference on where the Ground Check needs to go.

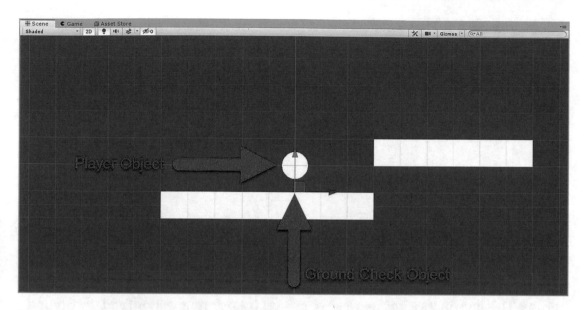

Figure 8-13. *Scene view showing the Ground Check placement*

Step 9

We now need to make some changes with our player script to function with our new Ground Check. Open your playerScript and add the following code highlighted in Bold:

```
public class playerScript : MonoBehaviour
{
    public float speed, jumpForce;
    public Rigidbody2D rb;
    public Transform groundCheck;
    bool grounded = false;

    void Start()
    {
        rb = GetComponent<Rigidbody2D>();
    }

    void Update()
    {
        float h = Input.GetAxisRaw("Horizontal");
```

```
grounded = Physics2D.Linecast(transform.position, groundCheck.
position, 1 << LayerMask.NameToLayer("Ground"));

transform.Translate(new Vector3(h * speed * Time.deltaTime, 0, 0));

if (Input.GetButtonDown("Jump") && grounded)
{
    rb.AddForce(new Vector2(0, jumpForce), ForceMode2D.Impulse);
}

    }
}
```

This will assign *grounded* the value of 1 or 0 (true or false) based on the outcome of the line. This line draws a line between our player (transform.position) and the Ground Check object (groundCheck.position). 1 << LayerMask.NameToLayer("Ground") ignores all Layers other than Ground. We will create the Ground layer shortly.

Step 10

To bring this tutorial to a close, we need to add a new layer to our tilemap for our Ground Check to work with the environment. Select the Tilemap object in the Hierarchy, and at the top of the Inspector, click the layer drop-down menu and select Add Layer. This is the same method we used for our 3D FPS project earlier in this book. But refer to Figure 8-14 for a recap.

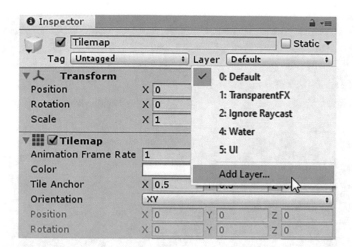

Figure 8-14. *Tilemap in the Inspector to change the Layer type*

In the User Layer 8 box, type "Ground" (it will need to be the same spelling as the NameToLayer line in our playerScript which was Ground!). See Figure 8-15.

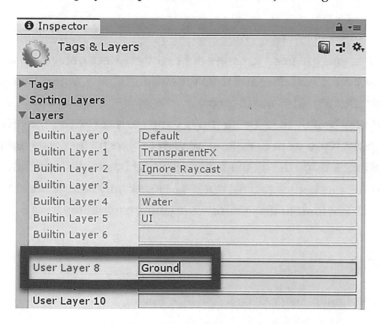

Figure 8-15. *Layer settings in the Inspector to create a new Ground layer*

Make sure that you select the tilemap object once more and assign the new layer you have just created as depicted in Figure 8-16.

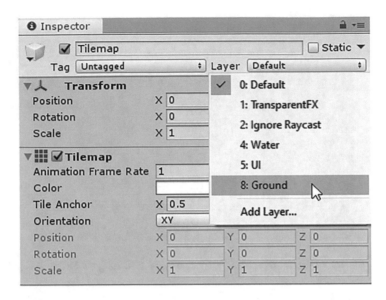

Figure 8-16. *Applying the Ground layer in the Tilemap Inspector*

Step 11

For your final step, you will need to assign our Ground Check object to our playerScript. Select the Player object, and drag and drop the Ground Check object from the Hierarchy into the Ground Check field in the Inspector.

You should now be able to test your project and see your player move left to right while also jumping! If you want to expand on your project further, why not try adding some more platforms using the tilemap so your player has something they can jump onto? Or add some mechanics such as double jump or only being able to move in a certain direction? The limit to these tutorials is your imagination!

Conclusion

So far within this chapter, we have covered the following:

1. Developing your skills further within programming and working with the X and Y axes

2. Considering directional movement within Unity

3. How to create tilemaps

4. Working with collisions within 2D

With our final practical tutorial completed, we now move into the final chapters of the book which will begin to cover what a HUD and UI mean in terms of game design and how we can create these. This will also branch into menus and accessibility options while also thinking about the most effective ways for your player to use menus during gameplay.

CHAPTER 9

HUD and UI. What Does It Mean?

We've all seen it and it works like muscle memory. When playing games, our eyes dart around the screen to look for the health or stamina bar to show us how our character is coping with combat or exploring. But as simple as it might be, the heads-up display, or known as the HUD, is the most effective way to communicate this information to the player. The key when it comes to designing elements of the HUD is to ensure that it is not cluttered, and everything is legible. But before we can investigate this, let's look at some of the most common elements that we see on our screens during playtime:

- Health bar

- Ammunition indicator

- Mini map or radar

- Stamina

- Reticule

- Levelling-up indicator

- Inventory

Reticule

Again, you may not even notice till you engage in combat, but the reticule appears in the very center of our screens when we play first-person shooter (FPS) games. Something so simple such as a dot or a target can help the player indicate their direction of movement or aim toward targets. But that is how it should be: simple. This element should not take over the screen nor should it be the focus for the player. While they are most common

© Michael Killick 2022
M. Killick, *The Way We Play*, https://doi.org/10.1007/978-1-4842-8789-7_9

within FPS games to appear on the screen for the duration of gameplay, they will also appear in third-person games while the player is aiming. When coloring the reticule, ensure that it can be always seen. If your game is set in a snowy landscape, then avoid making the reticule white so it blends in with the player's surroundings. Regarding coloring, make it clear who are friends or foe when aiming. FPS games tend to turn the reticule blue or green for friendlies or civilians, and enemies red. Danger will always be red! Some FPS games give the player the option to use aim assist and help the player lock onto targets quicker in a firefight. Some games even design the reticule to move toward a target to help the player aim toward their enemy. Players tend to be given the option if they would like aim assist depending on their preferred playstyle. In *Marvel's Avengers*, when the player is Captain America, they are given the chance to throw their shield at enemies or to help solve puzzles. When aiming, the player can use the reticule to aim toward multiple enemies to inflict damage. Who knew that a simple circle or dot on your screen could be so useful!

Ammo Indicator

There are typically two types of indicators for ammo: number or ammunition. One might suit the game better, but this will be down to the style of game you intend to make. As this is something that is going to be watched the most on a screen, this needs to be simple and easy to read. The *Halo* series uses a mixture of these elements depending on the weapon the player is using. However, the designers use percentages for energy-based weapons as if they were powered by batteries. Some fully automatic weapons will have the ammo indicator on the gun and almost at the center of the screen so the player can keep track of their ammo. If you are going for a typical FPS ammo indicator, then *Call of Duty* displays their ammo at the bottom right of the screen. However, the designers will use both number and bullet image for that added bit of flair.

Same as weapon ammo, any grenades or special items that can be used need to be displayed clearly and near the weapon ammo indicator. If the player can use multiple items in battle, give them a way to open the items and select which would be suitable for them. *Halo: Infinite* gives the player the option to switch grenades and which ability they can use, such as the grapple or deployable shield.

Health Bar

The literal lifeblood of a character, the health bar helps keep track of the player's health or lives. That's it! To put it in a more serious manner, the health bar indicates how close the character is to their death.

The health bar can also be the most creative element of the HUD as this can range from hearts, a bar, or percentages or can change colors depending on the amount of health the player has. But this can also work in the opposite direction. Rather than a health bar, the player could have a damage bar, where if it fills, the player will die. One focuses on not reaching zero, and the other focuses on not reaching the maximum number.

There are other games where health is represented in other ways, such as a shield bar which can regenerate. For example, in the *Halo* series, the Master Chief has a shield that acts as his health bar, but if depleted, he is vulnerable to attacks which could end up killing him. But this shield will regenerate once the player has taken cover and has not taken any damage for a short period of time. This method of health is becoming quite common in games such as the *Uncharted* series, *Ghost of Tsushima*, and the *Call of Duty* games. Some games will use a health bar to represent the player's health, and others will use a coloring method. This coloring method will see the screen becoming black and white if the player is close to death. Corners of the screen might also turn red in the process to indicate damage has been taken, but similarly to *Halo*, the player will regain health if no damage is taken for a short period of time.

Mini Map/Radar

Something I'm finding more useful with the more games I play, but the mini map is a staple point to watching your corners from enemies and assisting you with finding those hidden treasures. Some games use the mini map to help guide the player to a waypoint they have marked on the map. It might also give the distance, so the player knows how close they are to their destination. But make sure that anything on the map is clear for the player to see. The hint with this is "mini." While the player can open the pause menu to visit the world map, having locations and items highlighted on the mini map needs to be clear to see. *Red Dead Redemption 2* gave the player the option to change the size of the map for the assist if the player needed a wider view of the mini map. But what you want the player to see on your mini map will be down to you.

Alternately, using a radar system will simplify what appears on them, but also encourages exploration from the player. The *Halo* series uses a radar system where only enemies will appear on the map as red dots. This will be within a 25-meter radius of the player. In some cases, enemies will only appear on the map if they are making noise or have discharged their weapon, which provides their location for the player.

Regardless of which method you choose, you need to ensure that the player can still enjoy the gameplay without the mini map or radar being in the way. These work best if they appear in the bottom corners of the screen, tucked away but still easy enough for the player to refer to during their game time. If you decide to have different locations on your game map, ensure that there is a legend for the player to refer to. The worst thing to happen is give the player lots of different locations and them not understanding where they are going or who they might be seeing. This also goes for marking extra locations on the map. There might be some cool locations on a map the player might need to return to in the future, so why not give them the option to mark them on the map for their own reference?

The mini map can also provide lots of other help notions during gameplay, including an altitude indicator that is perfect for those that are flying low to the ground or water. *Grand Theft Auto 5* incorporates the indicator as soon as the player enters a flying vehicle. But it also acts as a depth indicator if the player enters a submarine. If the player dives too deep underwater, the submarine will start to take damage before the player is crushed to death. Morbid I know! But using these tricks for a mini map or radar is an excellent way for your game to be immersive and to expand your gameplay.

Stamina

Similar to the health bar, the stamina bar indicates how much stamina the player might have to carry out certain moves. In *The Elder Scrolls* series, the player is given three bars at the bottom of the screen: health, magic, and stamina. The player's stamina bar will reduce if the player runs, fights, or swims. Stamina, however, can be upgraded and provide the player with some extra energy if they need it in combat or exploration.

If the player has run out of stamina while playing, make it clear that this has happened. If the player loses stamina during combat, the character could slow or look tired while the player waits to regain stamina. The character could also use deep breathing to indicate they are tired. Be clever about how you tell the player that they need to rest.

If your game uses potions or times for the player to rest, these could be quick ways for stamina or even health regain. But try to give the player these options at suitable times. You wouldn't want your player to camp on the battlefield to regain health!

Levelling-Up Indicator

A bar that tends to be seen within menus or under player customization, but the levelling-up indicator shows the player's progress to achieving the next level of their character. Experience points (XP) might be awarded for missions, combat, collectibles, and more which will assist the player with unlocking more content and extras for their character. This indicator might appear on the screen but only when XP has been collected. *Destiny* shows a simple white bar at the bottom of the screen if the player has collected XP but will change color if the player has made it to the next level. These are great to design and can be tailored to the design of the character. For example, a levelling-up indicator might be red for a character who mainly wears red and blue for someone who mainly wears blue. But your game doesn't need to use XP. *Grand Theft Auto* uses RP (respect points) to level up the player while playing online. Their indicator appears at the top of the screen but at one end shows the level the player is on, and the other shows the level they will reach next. This helps give the player a target while they can also see how much RP they need to make it to the next level.

Inventory

A hallmark feature used within RPG and open-world games, the inventory is used to keep track of items and collectibles needed on the player's adventures. Players should be able to have quick access to items they have found to use in combat, missions, puzzles, etc. The inventory can typically be toggled by a button on your controller or keyboard to show the full list of collected items. An assigned item list might also appear on the screen to assist players with items they regularly use. *Minecraft* offers the player up to nine items to quickly select during their adventures, but these can be changed through the main inventory selection.

RPG games such as *Pokémon Legends: Arceus* and *The Elder Scrolls* series allow the player to carry a limited number of items and require them to store the rest of their treasures in an in-game house or chest. If this is something you decide to use, make sure that the player can carry their main items, but give them the choice to view everything they have collected on their adventures. However, *The Elder Scrolls* series incorporates a weight system, where certain items require more strength to carry and will limit the player to how much they can carry and how much will need to be stored elsewhere. Limiting your inventory will be up to you and the style of game you wish to use. If limiting it is something you wish to consider, make sure you give your player the chance to upgrade the size of their inventory to add some progression and goals they can achieve. Keeping it linear will make the gameplay tough, but giving flexibility will always swing in your favor!

Similarly, to an inventory, some first-person games give the player an item selection using the control pad on a controller (or assigned keys on a keyboard) that is specific to the level. These items or tools can be used for puzzles or key elements within missions.

Achievements (Honorable Mention)

Introduced with the Xbox 360 and PlayStation 3, trophies and achievements gave new goals for players to max out their game time. Microsoft took it a step further and awarded players with points or better known as Gamerscore. This is used as a social element to compete against friends to see who can collect the most Gamerscore each month. It can also be used to flex who has the highest and who has played the most games. The more difficult the achievement, the greater the Gamerscore. While Xbox had developed this, PlayStation has almost stayed the same with their trophy system from the PlayStation 3 through to the PlayStation 5. Trophies are graded on Bronze, Silver, and Gold, while each game will have a Platinum trophy for those that manage to collect all other trophies for a game. This can also be seen as a social element and comparable with friends.

While these can be fun to collect and share with friends, they offer the player a way to expand their gameplay and collect all trophies/achievements. This could be from delivering a special attack, finding a certain item, completing the game on a particular difficulty, or down to completing the main storyline. Achievements are an excellent way for the player to get the most out of their money and maximize their game time. If you decide to use achievements, make sure that they have flashy sounds and animations to make it clear that the player has achieved something. Xbox now have Diamond achievements which have a unique sound to tell the player they have achieved a special target. Both PlayStation and Xbox have percentages to give the player an idea on how many players achieve that trophy while playing the game.

Whatever UI elements you decide to use, there are three fundamental factors you need to consider when designing them:

- Size

- Placement

- Color

These pillars of all HUD design will ensure that your player can see what they have on their screen, will not interfere with their gameplay, and will be accessible for all.

Size

We have touched upon this briefly with the mini map, but what is the point of creating a UI element that is too small to see? There is nothing worse than a player having to sit nearer the screen to see a weapon selection or a mini map. Most games should be played in comfort (unless they require the player to get up and move!) and can be enjoyed without having to adjust where the player is sitting to see the game.

A game I recently played (for the purpose of the book, I shall not name which game it was) was a third-person action-shooter which required me to collect a range of weapons to shoot oncoming aliens. While the gameplay was fast paced and required lots of guns for different enemies, being able to use the weapon wheel to change guns required me to sit nearer the screen to see what I was doing. At times, I found myself squinting at the screen to see what I was choosing. If you are going to make a weapon selection, make sure the player can easily see it. If the player is in combat and requires them to change weapons for certain enemies, you could add a slow-time feature to give them a chance to change to what they need. Alternatively, make the player open a menu which pauses the game to select a weapon. This will give them time to take a breath and work on tactics if they are caught in a boss fight.

Placement

If the HUD element is in the way of the gameplay, then you know it is not in the correct place! Making sure that your screen isn't cluttered with these elements is key for the player to focus on what they are doing in-game. Whatever elements you decide to use for your game, ensure that they are strategically placed on the screen. For example, health bars tend to appear in the top left of the screen and ammunition indicator in the bottom right. If mini maps are used, they might be in the bottom left of the screen, or a horizontal compass style map could be seen in the top middle. Do your research and play games of a similar genre to which you would like to make. See what other designers have created and methods they have used. Play some games and see what works for you!

Color

I briefly mentioned the word accessibility when it comes to the coloring of your HUD elements. Like the size of your HUD, you need to choose a color that can be seen against the gameplay. Any colours you choose for your game need to be seen by everyone with impairments such as dyslexia or sight. *The Last of Us Part 2* was hailed as one of the most accessible games created due to the extensive accessible settings developed for the players. This included the size and color of subtitles, menus, HUD elements, as well as sound and visual cues to help when the player engaged in combat.

In the game I recently played in which I struggled with the size of the HUD, I also struggled with the chosen color for the HUD. It was a deep blue, and while it was a nice shade of blue, it was almost impossible to see when I was walking across fields or in brightly lit temples. A white- or gray-colored HUD would have worked more effectively for this game and would have made it easier to see the health and the ammo indicator.

Also, carry out your research when thinking about colors and the HUD. Knowing what works best with other colors and the theme of your game is crucial to designing an accessible game and a clear and concise HUD.

Static and Dynamic HUD

Some games don't use a HUD, or they use something called a dynamic or a static HUD. A dynamic HUD is where the HUD will disappear if the player isn't interacting with what they have on the screen, such as reloading or healing. A static HUD stays on the screen for the duration of the gameplay, except for cutscenes and main menus. This is normally the easiest of the two HUD styles to design as you need to decide what will be shown on the screen, such as health, ammo, stamina, etc. Once they decide, they will be with the player forever!

Dynamic HUDs are typically used if you are trying to convey an immersive experience and for the player to engross themselves within the gameplay. Most third-person exploration games will use a dynamic HUD to maximize the screen space so the player can see more of the game world. But there are a few key notes to consider if this is the option you wish to go with:

- Some games have started to include optional dialogue for the player to learn more about the characters and develop upon the story further. While these are optional, you will need to give the player a prompt to show that these conversations can take place. An icon of a controller button might appear above the character's head in a speech bubble to indicate they have something to say.

- This can also be used if the player needs to carry out an activity such as moving an object with a side character to progress further in the level. This could also be another speech bubble or a sound prompt, so the player knows what to do next.

- Some levers, switches, doors, or key items within the world might glow to inform the player that they need to approach and interact with them. *Halo: Infinite* uses an IR scanner (infrared) to scan the field for key items and a waypoint to the next area to go. This will light up the screen bright yellow and leaves a marker to show the direction and distance from the next area.

But What If I Want It All?

What if your game needs a static HUD that is tracking health, power of weapons, mini map, stamina of an animal you are riding, inventory, number of throwable items, armor health, distance to next mission, player progress, and so much more? You would typically find this style of HUD in MMORPGs (massively multiplayer online role-playing games) such as *League of Legends* or *World of Warcraft*. When it comes to tracking all these aspects, simplicity is key. There are a lot of things for the player to look at as well as concentrate on the gameplay itself. So, what is the best method for it? I have narrowed it down to the main points to consider if you ever see yourself designing a HUD for an MMORPG game in your future, or if your game ends up with a busy HUD where the player will need to concentrate on various elements of your world:

- Make your most important buttons easy to see and reach. If your player is in combat and needs to heal, make the button easy to see and placed somewhere the player can reach for those extra health points. Don't make them search through a main menu or inventory to find those potions!

- If you are working with artists, let them work on the designing of icons or buttons; they will have more experience in this area than dedicated programmers! Sometimes, it is better to leave some aspects to the professionals!

- If you are going to use icons, choose the right image to represent the following action. If you are going to heal the player, the icon could be a heart. If you are going to reload your weapon, the icon might be three bullets with arrows circling it. If the player clicks an icon, make sure that there is a sound or cue to tell them they were successful or not with their actions, which leads us into the next item.

- Interactive adaptive audio (IAA) – If the player interacts with something on the menu, world, or HUD, make it known that they have done so. Giving feedback to the player will tell them if they are doing right or wrong with their actions. When playing the original *Pokémon* games, the game gives the player a "thud" noise when they walk into something. This tells them that they cannot move any further.

- Coloring your icons to match their intentions or abilities helps give the player an indication of what they will do. Various moves in the *Pokémon* series are colored to match their type. Fire moves are colored red/orange, dark types are black, water are blue, ice types are light blue, and so on. If you want to go the extra mile to help your player, you could show stats of what the moves or items are resistant to when combating others.

- As mentioned, keeping it simple is crucial; no one wants to read paragraphs of text during intense moments in your game to heal their character. But if you want to guide your player further and maybe even remind them of what each button does, have a small text above an icon if the player places their cursor over it. A reminder is always helpful.

Where Do These Things Go Anyway?

It's one thing to learn about the different elements within a HUD, but it's another to think about their placement on a screen. While we have mentioned this earlier in the chapter, we will now think about the effectiveness of placement and what will work best when it comes to the decision making.

If you think about a third-person game and your character is standing in the middle of the screen, this area will now be off limits for any icons or HUD elements to appear here, except for any reticules or small text to identify game objects. You want to ensure that nothing will obscure the action, so keep the middle free! Some menus will pause the gameplay but also have a translucent menu so the player can still see the player. This can be handy if you are called for dinner and want to pick up where you left off!

When thinking about typical game screens, health, armor, and any stats will typically appear in the top left or bottom left of the screen. It could also appear in the top middle! This is normally where the most important information during gameplay will be. *God of War PS4* has its health in the bottom left which also shows any runes and abilities the player can use, and *Ratchet & Clank* has its health and player progression in the top middle. A good reason for this is that some parts of the world will read from left to right. So, moving your eyes from health to action can feel normal for some.

Sometimes, the bottom of the screen will also be home to some icons or HUD elements. While a world compass might feature on the outside edge of a mini map, games such as *The Elder Scrolls* series use a rectangular compass to show waypoints. This could be placed at the top middle or bottom middle of the screen. However, placing elements in these places can be a tricky move. You need to ensure that they will always appear on the screen and avoid any clipping. Some older televisions or monitors may not be to the same aspect ratio your game was created in, which could lead to some of your HUD appearing off screen. Work out a place on the screen that works best for your game but also avoids any possibility of being cut off. More recent games give the player the option to adjust their game's settings so menus and HUDs will always fit with their monitor's resolution. If this isn't a feature you are going to add, it's worth testing your HUD with different monitors just to be sure that everything works smoothly!

Sometimes, less is more! Try to convey as much information to the player as possible in as little HUD elements as you can. If you end up having health in the top left; the mini map in the bottom left; ammo, abilities, and weapons in the bottom right; and any supporting character's health and stats in the top right, then the screen will feel really crowded. There are a couple of ways to avoid this. Either give the player the option to customize their HUD to whatever suits their playstyle (giving players freedom is something they always love to have!) or double up on some elements rather than having them as multiple. For example, health and stamina are bars that sit under each other but given different colors to identify which is which. Whatever you do, make sure that the player doesn't feel overwhelmed the moment they start playing and trying to understand everything on the screen. The HUD should be treated like a language. Teach the player what each element means until they can decipher what it means and how they can best use it for their game over time. The more they use the HUD, the better the understanding will be of it. *God of War PS4* doesn't give the player the compass element until two hours into gameplay, so you can take your time introducing elements to the player!

As I mentioned earlier in this section, you can give the player a chance to upgrade armor or weapons during action so they can have the upper hand in combat. But the choice on whether you want the player to think about their upgrades before they go into action is up to you. You can do this by not letting the game pause during combat if the player needs to change their weapons or craft a certain item in their inventory while combat is taking place. This means the player will need to act fast to avoid being killed. This will also encourage them to always be prepared. *The Last of Us* series do not offer this function as they want their audience to feel suspense during a firefight. So, if the player is injured, they need to take cover while they heal themselves or craft an item.

If the player needs to find an item in their inventory, open a menu, or change a gameplay option, this should always be easy! There is nothing worse than having to navigate their way through four menus, to find something that will help them with their game. Something should always be within reach. You wouldn't want to walk into another room on a different floor of your house to change the TV channel, so why make your play go on a scavenger hunt for something that could help them or improve their experience? If the player needs to open a map, it should be as easy as a single button press. The quicker the player can find something, the happier they will be!

A Note on Menus

Other than HUD, we now need to consider looking at the UI (user interface) within a game. I could spend hours and chapters talking to you about all the games I have played that have used great menus which were clear, bright, and simple, and those that just really weren't great to use or see. But I want to walk you through each section of a menu so you can see some of the effective ways to design them (I have tried to put them in order that you would see them when loading a game):

- Splash screens

- Legal information

- Title screen

- Options

- Save/load game file

- Loading screen

- Pause menu

- Controls

- Credits

Splash Screens

Remember when you load up a game and you see lots of fancy animations and sounds for company logos. These are splash screens that show the player the companies behind the game. For legal reasons, all parties need to be shown and given credit for their work and involvement within the project

Legal Information

There might be a few legal screens to show important information about the game and the company, but players commonly skip these screens. This is for companies and manufacturers to share legal information about the game you are about to play. While this isn't a legal feature, some games will have a side note that encourages the player to take regular breaks and avoid playing games for a lengthy amount of time. Whether you listen to this advice is up to you, but it is always beneficial to take a break rather than sitting down for hours on end – whether you are designing or playing games!

Title Screen

Once all the legal stuff has been shown and all the disclaimers, the title screen will be the first thing the player sees before they jump straight into the game. First impressions are hard to erase, so getting this right is crucial! You want to create something that will capture the player before they make it to the main menu. Whether you achieve this through intense music or an introductory cinematic scene which sets the story, this will set the tone for your game and get the player excited. While the player will see the box art when purchasing the game, the title screen will set the tone. But the way you design it will be up to you:

- You can be minimalistic with your approach. *Uncharted 4* keeps the menu simple and short. The menu is at the bottom left of the screen so the player can see a dead pirate swinging in a cage from a tree. The player knows immediately that this is going to focus on pirates and will be in a jungle.

- You can go for a classic menu approach with the main game logo in the middle and the menu options below as a list. Games such as *Super Mario Bros*, *God of War*, the *Lego* series, and *Minecraft* all use this approach.

- Sometimes, gameplay or animations are shown while navigating through the menu. While gameplay isn't shown during this menu, *Marvel's Avengers* shows the roster of characters in the game once the player reaches the menu. The cool thing with this is when the player changes an outfit for a character, the player can see it immediately on the character in the menu. The problem with having gameplay or animations in a menu is that it can get too busy. If someone who is new to games and wants to navigate through the menu to set up audio, visual, or controls, seeing animations in the background can be off-putting. Keep it simple and don't distract the player too much from navigating through your well-designed menu!

A hidden feature within a title screen which used to feature in older generation games is if the game was in an idle state for too long, the official game trailer would play. Once shown, the game would return to the menu. But this will become a cycle if the player leaves the game in an idle state until they pick up their controller. *Lego Star Wars: The Complete Saga* was famous for this and would show its trailer to those that would leave the menu running until the player interacts with it!

Options

A gray area within menu design is the options menu. While I've advised you to keep your menus simple, creating an options menu is going to contradict everything I have said about them so far! When games started out, there were no such things as an options menu. Just play, high score, and quit. As time passed, games became more complex and offered players a plethora of options to customize their playstyle. Typical options were adjusting the audio and visual aspect of the game to work with powerful monitors or home speaker systems, but now players can change buttons on keyboards and controllers to match peripherals they use, such as a gaming mouse or Pro Controllers (a controller that has extra buttons and can be customized for those that play competitively). But something that has become increasingly common is the incorporation of accessible settings (something that will be covered later in this chapter). As a roundup, make sure that your menu can be easily navigated and broken down into subsections your player can navigate:

- Audio

- Visual

- Gameplay

- Controls

- Game extras (for those that can purchase cheats or game enhancers such as infinite ammo or health)

Save/Load Game

Something that should be straightforward and simple is being able to load and save your game files. Some games have limits to the amount of save files there can be, and some have an unlimited amount. The best advice I can give when it comes to this is give the player the chance to create their first game save file once they have selected their difficulty (if you have this in the game). If you don't give them the option to create their save file before they begin the game, the unthinkable could happen and they forget to manually save their game after an hour in before they switch off. It happens, but you can be the one to stop this from happening!

When you load up a save file, it might show the location where the player last saved, their playtime, date they last played, and sometimes their overall game completion percentage. Having this can be a nice touch for the player to remind themselves on how well they are getting on with the game. Sometimes, it can be a pat on the back if they see a save file with 100% completion written on it!

Give the player the option to delete their save files if they would like to. But give them some disclaimers before they confirm they want to delete their progress. There is nothing worse than to press delete by mistake and lose everything they have been working on! It is also worth considering the amount of save file slots that a game can have. If a family is wanting to play the same game, family members might want their own save file to have their own adventure. Typically, there might be three to six save slots on a game. But others might only have one. The main *Pokémon* series only offers the player one save file, which means they will need to delete their data if they wish to play the story again!

New Game+ is a feature where the player can play the game again from the start but play it on the next level of difficulty. Collectibles and upgrades will be carried over to help them with the next difficulty level. If this is something you choose to add, make sure that the player doesn't override their original save, but saves it into a free space. The great thing about a New Game+ is that there are things in the first playthrough that the player is unable to unlock, unless they play through the game again. This encourages replayability which is always a bonus to have!

Loading Screen

Something the player will always fail to skip out of impatience is the loading screen. We have all seen one, whether it be in applications, software, or games; it's these that we hate to see and would remove if given the chance.

However, as we now move into more powerful technology, the loading screen is something that is becoming a thing of the past. But it is always beneficial to include them if the player needs to see something while the game loads. Typical loading screens will feature artwork and maybe some tips on how to use abilities and reminders of the story. How you decide to fill this gap is up to you:

- *The Elder Scrolls: Skyrim* shows player models and some trivia from the game story while the game loads. The player can read about the models while also learning about the lore of the game. *Lego Star Wars: The Skywalker Saga* shows miniature ships from the game and stats about them while the game is loading.

- *Pokémon Shining Pearl* and *Brilliant Diamond* show the started Pokémon in the bottom right of the screen jumping while the player waits, while *Pokémon Legends: Arceus* shows a player running animation in the same place.

- *The Last of Us* series uses butterflies and fireflies while the game loads. While this isn't obvious from the start, these are subtle nods to the game story the player will learn about.

- Showing concept art is always a good option as there are some players out there who play games based on the artwork. You never know, you might inspire someone to create artwork based on the style you have used!

- Google Chrome uses this while the user waits for their Internet to connect, but they have added in a 2D side scrolling game. Having a minigame to play while you wait is a good idea instead of your player staring at a screen while their game loads. But be mindful of how long it takes to play the minigame. If the player is still playing it when the game has loaded, make a button appear on the screen so they have the option to leave the minigame and continue with the main game.

Top Tip   Have something animated on the screen while the game is loading. If your screen is static, then the player will struggle to know if the game has crashed during loading!

Pause Menu

The chance to give the player a break from the game; the pause menu needs to be clear but also offers the option to save progress, access the game map, change any options, or access the inventory. As mentioned earlier, you can give the option here during the design phase if you would like gameplay to continue while the pause menu is active or typically pause everything for the player. Like the options menu, there are various menus the player can access from a pause menu:

- Options

- Bonus material

- Cheat codes

- Credits

- Difficulty settings

- Save/load game

- Exit game

In *God of War PS4*, when in the pause menu, it brings the player to the customization tab where changes to appearance, weapons, and abilities can be made. The player can use L1 or R1 to cycle through the different tabs such as settings, world map, perks, armor, skills, goals, codex, and resources. All expand the gameplay in their own way, and everything can change the experience the player has with the game.

Controls

If the player needs to change their control or even see them as a recap, then make sure they can see a visual to help. Showing a controller or keyboard which indicates the controls to the player will give a visual reference. It's worth considering giving the player the option to customize their controls if they would like to make any changes.

In some third-person games, when a player has unlocked a new skill, a short animation will play to show what will happen and the controls needed to make it work. New skills and abilities will need to be shown so the player has reference to them for the future.

Credits

While some see these as boring and want to skip them, this should be a celebration of the hard work from everyone who has had an input into the game. Everyone who has had an involvement from production, art, animating, marketing, and even down to testing should have their names in the spotlight. Make sure that everyone has their name in the game credits. Even if there have been disputes or disagreements or someone has provided an input into the game, then their name should be featured. Names deserve to be seen, and this should be entertaining to watch. Whether it is down to incredible music, extra cutscenes, or more gameplay, players should be encouraged to stick around through the credits. The *Halo* series does it perfectly by allowing players who have completed the game on the highest difficulty to have a special credit cutscene as a reward for players. *Guardians of the Galaxy* also does it brilliantly by including the game's final boss fight during the credits. Just to make sure the player is giving their attention!

Scoring/Stats (Honorable Mention)

Telltale Games perfected this with their story-based games. Players would be given crucial choices through their stories which would impact how their story unfolds. Once a chapter is completed, the player would see the stats made based on other player's choices. This might show the percentage of those that chose to go down a secret path, or kept a character alive, but this was a great way to reflect upon what has happened so far. Just make sure that this isn't boring. Anyone can read percentages or scores, but make it interesting to read. Why not have images from your choices so the player can reflect on what happened when they made it, or make it appear like a storyboard and tell the chapter again?

If a story game isn't something you are going to make, but would like to have a score screen, here are a few things you could show your player:

- Score

- Enemies defeated

- Time taken for completion

- Items found

- Times killed

- Hints used

- Number of lives

- Objectives completed

- Secrets found

This can also be used as bragging rights; make sure your player can show off their progress to their mates if they see it!

Accessibility in Games

It's been mentioned a few times now within this chapter, but it's time to explore it further. Accessibility within game design is something which is becoming more common as technology is changing and evolving. This is the understanding of making games accessible and inclusive, so everyone of all backgrounds and impairments can enjoy games and experience them as fully as the next person.

It is vital that we aim to understand and support as many players as possible in accessing games. Games were designed to enjoy, so why should others face barriers when wanting to have fun?

Case Study: *The Last of Us Part 2*

2020 saw the release of one of the most anticipated game sequels, a follow-up to 2013's multiaward-winning *The Last of Us*. In addition to excellent gameplay, a heartfelt story, and great design, developer Naughty Dog also implemented the largest suite of accessibility tools seen in any game so far. To get an idea on what I am referring to, I have provided a list of some of the settings that have been used to review as follows:

- HUD rescaling

- Screen magnifier

- Camera distance from the character

- Navigation assistance

- Infinite abilities (such as holding breath underwater and ammunition)

- Text to speech

- Audio combat cues

- Change in difficulty for a range of aspects, such as enemies, resources, stealth, and overall game difficulty

- Traversal audio cues

As mentioned, this was just a small list of the settings they developed for the game. Now as you have reviewed the list, have a think about how the features support gamers. Think about the barriers that are currently present in games, if and how these features will help them access gameplay, and any other thoughts you have about the solution. It will also be worth doing your research to learn more about the settings that were used within the game to help you with this task.

When designing video games, on the surface, it might appear that you need to draw the art, program the game, design the menus, record the music and sounds, and animate the characters. But there are different areas within accessibility that need to be considered to ensure that all can access your game. Here are the main groups:

- Motor

- Cognitive

- Vision

- Hearing

All come with their own barriers, but also solutions on how players from all backgrounds can still enjoy the game you have designed. There are also some tips on what you can do to support players when designing your game.

Motor

How we typically play games is by using a controller, mouse, keyboard, steering wheel, pedals, and more. But there are those that have reduced mobility and require diverse needs to support them with playing games. When developing and designing games, options should be there to ensure that those with mobility impairments can still enjoy your game.

- Games that use one touch on a phone, keyboard, or controller can be a great way to play games, as some players may not be able to hold a controller or reach the full length of a keyboard to press buttons in combinations.

- Some games require players to hold down a key to destroy an item or turn levers to open a door. Try to avoid this and change it to a tap action. Restricted mobility can make it difficult to hold down buttons for long periods of time.

- Reduced gameplay difficulty should be adjustable for those that cannot play for long periods. Players might have low stamina and cannot focus to carry out repetitive movements such as combat. Being able to reduce or change difficulty can still offer the same gameplay experience for players.

- Make functions of a game accessible, such as photo mode (the function of being able to take photos in-game). Players should be able to enjoy playing without the need for support when they are having fun. There is nothing more frustrating than to ask for help while stuck on a screen or not being able to use a function in the game.

Cognitive

This covers a wide range of experiences for players, such as dyslexia, memory loss, and sometimes motion sickness (this can happen frequently when playing virtual reality games). So relaying information about the game's story, mechanics, and anything that is useful for the player to know is crucial so they can get the full experience of your game.

- Avoid anything that flashes with intensity. Those that have photosensitivity might suffer from strobe lighting or flickering images. This should be something that can be adjusted or switch off depending on the needs of the player.

- Having a clean HUD and UI helps managing and reading icons on a screen much easier. If you have followed everything in this chapter so far, then this one should be easy for you!

- If designing a text-based game, make sure that the player has enough time to read and take in all the information that is needed, but also ensure that it is legible. It should be that the fonts can be changed for those with dyslexia; this should be adjustable within the options menu.

- If a player suffers from memory loss, then being able to review controller maps or revisiting tutorials to learn the controls will make things much easier. While practicing of mechanics and mastering them is vital during gameplay, having the option to review controls in their own time will be helpful.

- Any motion blur or any other motion effects can be adjusted or switched off. Having the option to reduce it can still provide the original experience, but giving the player an option is beneficial to them.

Vision

While all impairments that we have covered so far are a challenge to live with, designing a game for those who have limited vision or blind shouldn't be a challenge.

- Being able to adjust the contrast is excellent. Some players with eyestrain may need these settings adjusted for a better experience. Being able to invert colors or having the option to change the lighting is also a great idea.

- Most horror games will use lighting to create atmosphere and set the tone of the game. But those with limited sight may not be able to distinguish objects in the world. Lighting should always be an option that can be adjusted.

- Audio description is a commonly used feature for television, but it is now becoming more common within video games. Using this for cutscenes is still a great way for your player to experience what is happening through the story outside of the gameplay. This can also be used when navigating menus to identify buttons or icons on the screen.

- When thinking about level design and designing the gameplay, you will need to consider what will make the game easier to complete. The player could start with more health, reduced health on enemies, the paths through levels are colour coded to show the main path through the environment and aim assist when engaging in combat. *The Last of Us 2* used a method of visual and nonvisual cues to tell the player when there is an enemy getting closer. Vibrations could be felt in the controllers which would intensify as enemies drew near. The speaker in the DualShock controller would also play sound effects to inform the player of what is happening in the world around them or when an action has been carried out.

Hearing

Creating immersion is through the designing of sound and visual. But if you take one away, players still deserve to experience your game to its fullest.

- Another common feature that would be seen on television is subtitles. Games typically have subtitles switched on at the start of a game and are normally kept on for a player's preference. I know I like to use them to make sure that I don't miss anything that has been said in the story, and I don't require any support for my hearing. But these subtitles should be adjusted to support visual-based players too. This can be from a range of sized fonts, colored text backgrounds, and colored fonts.

- If your game incorporates enemies patrolling the world, have an indicator to tell the player they are getting close to an enemy or an enemy is sneaking up on the player. Also, show if the player is making any noise in the world which could alert enemies. This is used in most exploration or stealth games and will be shown with an indicator that would change color if the player has been noticed or has aroused suspicion with an enemy.

- Vibrations can also be used to indicate distance of enemies, weapons being fired, explosions, or vehicles driving past.

While the preceding list is simply informing you of these areas, it is always important to do your research and learn about what can be done to support gamers out there. If there are ever times when you are unsure of what you can do to make your game accessible, speak to those that know best. There are plenty of charities that support those that wish to play games or even speak to those that struggle with barriers. Getting firsthand advice and suggestions is invaluable.

Never be afraid to reach out to someone who supports accessibility within games or those that have a field in designing accessible games. Being inclusive is the moral and right thing to do and should be considered by all designers.

Conclusion

So far within this chapter, we have covered the following:

1. What does the HUD and UI mean in terms of game design?

2. What elements are there of the HUD and how can we design them?

3. What is accessibility in games, and how can we consider it?

4. How to make an effective menu?

5. Games that have created effective menus

As we now move to the final chapter of the book, we will now consider some of the best things to avoid during game design. While this book has provided the best tips and tricks to start you out on your journey, or even help you during your journey, we now need to think about common mistakes and pitfalls of the process. There is never a right way to do something, but this next chapter will help you avoid issues and may even save you some time in the long run!

CHAPTER 10

Parting Advice

As we start to come to our journey's end, we have covered lots of aspects within game design that will help us use our time effectively while also considering what makes a game, well, a game. This has come from analyzing previous and well-known video games and identifying aspects that have been effective at either making them immersive or fun and what we could do to make them better or what would fit into our ideas.

But what are some final tips and advice before you begin or develop further within your design journey? While there are things that we do that work best for us and the way we work, there are some key mistakes that are common within the game design world that we will explore together.

Giving the player a break – Give the player time to relieve from intense moments in the game. This could be after a boss battle or an intense action scene that required skill and concentration. I always find that after moments like that, I need to take a breather to review my inventory and how many items I have left after that action sequence and sometimes listen to any interactions the protagonist has with any side characters about where the story will take the player next. Try not to let the player feel any burnout from moving into one battle to another. Action and intense moments should have peaks and troughs. During those troughs, the player should be able to explore the world around them for any missing collectibles or complete any side quests (if they appear in your game). I call this the "Smell the Grass" effect. This should be the period where the player can take in the world around them and take note on what they need to do next. During the peaks, this should be where the action or any combat takes place.

Testing the project – It might seem like a no-brainer, but what is the point of making a game if you don't test it during the development phase? With any practical development you make, whether it be a mechanic being implemented, edits to the environment, or sound effects generated, everything must be tested. This is where QA testing takes place to ensure that the game is working smoothly. During this period, the game will need to be tested to its limits to see if everything works and has been implemented correctly. The *Assassin's Creed* series have always been remarkably popular with their historic stories

M. Killick, *The Way We Play*, https://doi.org/10.1007/978-1-4842-8789-7_10

and their stealth mechanics. But one game in the series has been branded as one of the weaker ones, *Assassin's Creed: Unity*. The reason for this was character models were not rendering properly in-game; the player was falling through the floor and was plagued with bugs and glitches. And this was due to one important thing: a lack of testing! Due to this, players ridiculed the game and refused to play it as it was "unplayable." The game has since been updated and all glitches have been amended, and it is in the state it should have been from launch day. But players are quick to remember that a lack of testing and attention to detail was to blame for the game's downfall.

Testing isn't just for the developers to see if aspects of a game work, it is also used as part of marketing. Some big-name franchises such as *Call of Duty* have open beta testing for customers who preorder the latest title. This allows players to review the game before release and for players to decide if they wish to commit to purchasing the game. During which, players can also provide feedback online on what they thought of the title which the developers can use before the final release. This large-scale beta testing is seen more with triple A titles, but beta testing is also used with some indie games. While testing is advertised online to help with marketing for an upcoming release, the perfect place to gather feedback on a game is at video game exhibitions. One of the largest expos in the world that you might be familiar with is E3 (Electronic Entertainment Expo). Hosted in Los Angeles, this expo acts as the main stage for companies such as Sony, Microsoft, Bethesda, Nintendo, and many more giants within the industry. But it also plays home to smaller companies that wish to gather feedback on their projects. If you ever find yourself in a position to exhibit a project, try looking at some other expos such as EuroGamer Expo (EGX), Penny Arcade Expo (PAX), or Games Con. All offer developers a chance to share their work and the perfect place to network with others in the industry. Always be willing to share your work with others, you never know the feedback you might get!

Being too ambitious – Something I see on a yearly basis is when new developers begin designing a project that is near to the scale of *The Legend of Zelda* or another large game that they know and love. But they never understand, at first, the amount of time and skill that is needed to make a large-scale project for their first game.

Of course, it is great to be ambitious and aim high, but you also need to think about the realistic expectations of yourself and your team (if you are working in a team). Make sure that you play off your and your team's strengths. Also, chat with them to find out their skills and what they are capable of (you would typically ask this when you first work with someone new and see what their skills are). Always remember, you need to walk before you can run. And once you are running, then you can start to think about making larger projects!

Communication – Just as important as knowing and understanding games, having the equipment and the basic skills to make a game is to have good communication skills. If you don't talk to developers, your team, or a publisher, then how will you make or release your game? If you fail to speak to your team about development, then the game plan will fail. If you fail to speak to your publisher about details on the game, then the game will never be released. Notice a common word there? Fail! Failure to communicate will lead to failure within your game and your team. I have seen this core element fail many times and all because team members are not sharing their ideas or speaking to their team.

I was once overseeing a project where there were two artists creating artwork for a game. But both had ended up creating artwork for the same part of the game. And this was due to them not communicating and not having a clear plan on who is creating what. A decision couldn't be made on which design to use for the game. And you can probably imagine the difficult chat was made there! But this could have been avoided if they had been chatting to each other about responsibilities and task lists. You can use different methods to keep track of progress but also communication within a team. There are many platforms out there to manage this, and I have provided a list of them in Chapter 11.

Playing games – It might seem another no-brainer, but playing games for research is important to understand other genres and mechanics within a game. As I mentioned previously in this book, being able to play other genres outside of your comfort zone is the best way to understand how other games are made and what they feel like. For example, if someone plays more action/adventure games and little horror, they will need to explore more games such as *Outlast, Dead Space, Resident Evil*, and *Alien: Isolation* to get a better understanding of their themes before they can begin to create a horror game of their own. Another useful method to use is to review previous feedback from other players but also from the press. Having a range of opinions from different players and reviewers will help identify what audiences have enjoyed and what could have been better. There is no better place to get advice and feedback than from experience!

Rewards – Is there a point to doing something if there is no reward or pat on the back for completing a task? Some people might get a sense of achievement for completing a task, but others would like to see a reward for overcoming a challenge.

As a reiteration of a previous topic we have covered, rewarding the player for overcoming a challenge or reaching a certain point in a game will help them continue with playing. You need to entice the player to continue their journey by rewarding them with customization items or weapons that will help them on their journey. If they have been able to defeat a flaming boss in the pits of a volcano, reward them with a flaming sword that can set their enemies on fire. Make them feel like the boss they have just defeated! During gym battles in the *Pokémon* series, the gym leader will always use a powerful move against your team. Once you have defeated the gym leader, you are rewarded with that powerful move that you can use for your team.

The player should feel a sense of empowerment as they progress through the game. As they venture into difficult territory, the player should feel that they are skilled and a good match for whatever they face. If your game has a shop or marketplace where the player can purchase or upgrade gear with in-game currency, have certain items unlocked once they have reached a certain point in the game, or they have completed a collection challenge. Once the player has unlocked some awesome-looking armor that will help them in their quest, they should walk away from that shop feeling awesome and ready for anything. There's that sense of empowerment!

Gameplay before story – Do pictures come before the writing of the story? Or are they formed as the story develops? This is just like implementing a story into a game, but the gameplay must come first.

When designing a game, the story will be decided at the start during the design phase with the mechanics, characters, weapons, etc. (refer back to Chapter 1 for the creation of a GDD!), but when it comes to developing a prototype and preparing a project, the story must come afterward. The reason for this is that you need to start creating something that the player can experience and, more importantly, play. Design elements such as the story, sound, and menus will have their moment during the playthrough and in the development stage.

Another reason for this is that you were to attend an expo or a pitch, the audience will want to experience something to play. If a player has queued for hours to play your game at an expo, you know they will have been waiting to play something, and the story will come second to them while they are experiencing the demo.

In some cases, I have overseen some projects where the designers will come up with a detailed story with side quests, a plethora of characters, and multiple endings, but ran out of time to bring any of this to life. Balance your time wisely and ensure that you have something playable before you begin adding in your story.

Pride – Something that developers sometimes fail to do, and that is taking pride in the work that they have produced. I have seen two versions of this take place in design:

- Not taking pride – Some designers I have seen have created incomplete projects and didn't really show the effort during their development stage. They didn't show the drive to make a project, and, in the end, it didn't work out for them. As I have said many times before, you need to be a fan of the work you are producing and create it for the right reasons. Don't ever do something as you feel you have to, but do something because you want to. You should take pride in the work you do as ultimately it will affect your career progression if others don't see you working to your fullest.

- Not showing pride – You should be proud of the work you have produced and show the world your achievements. If you have been able to produce something that you are proud of and you have been able to achieve a personal goal, then you should be able to tell everyone what you have done. The constant use of sharing the work you have made will ultimately expand your portfolio and demonstrate your abilities to others. It is a big world out there within game design, and it is only going to get bigger, so you want to start showing everyone what you can do. Show pride in the work you produce and share your achievements!

Stick to your plans – When pitching and designing your game, you will create a GDD that will outline everything you wish to make for your game. But there are those that have a habit of changing plans during development which change the course of the game. While plans can change slightly, make sure that nothing changes completely. If there are features that you wish to add to the game, try adding them in but avoid affecting the player's overall experience.

Scraping projects and commitment – Similar to the previous tip, make sure that you are showing commitment with the project you are working on. Whether you are working solo or with a team, you need to ensure that you are sticking with the original idea and seeing it through to the end. If you and your team are excited about the project you are making, then you will do well with designing it.

The other scenario that I have seen is when a team scraps a project mid-development. This isn't something alien to happen in the industry, and it could have happened for a few different reasons, lack of money or team, time constraints, or the game hasn't been well received during test plays. But if you ever find yourself scrapping or taking a break from a project that you are working on, always keep it as you may return to it in the future.

Seeking help – Something I have seen on many occasions within game development is when someone or a team feels that they can achieve their goals without following advice from others. Please do not do this! If someone reviews your work or provides you with some advice, there is a good chance that they are right and will only make your project even better.

I had been overseeing a game project where a developer had been working on their own and juggling all of the roles that a team would have. After many conversations about managing their time and taking on a large amount of work for themselves, I advised them to seek some help from an artist to assist with their workload. Unfortunately, this developer stuck to their guns and wanted to create this game entirely on their own. While some developers want to do this (and this isn't a problem!), they struggled to complete their work on time and missed their deadline. It was a shame as their idea was starting to take form and looked like it could have been a very strong and fun project to play. But if they had taken the advice and sought help, things might have ended up differently.

Just be sure that if you ever find yourself struggling with something, be sure to seek help from those around you. There is never a problem with asking for help!

Do not rush your plans – There is nothing worse than to play a game that has been rushed. Showing a close attention to detail will not only show that your game has been made carefully and with care but also shows that you take your time with your efforts and want to show pride in the work you create. I have seen many rushed projects that end up missing crucial elements of the game, and they fail to test their final product, which in turn leads to an unplayable game. Take your time with anything you create and show a close attention to detail. You will forever be grateful to yourself for the extra time and effort you put into your work when someone loves what they see or play!

Conclusion

So far within this chapter, we have covered the following:

1. What things can you do to avoid during your game's design?

2. How you can better yourself and support your team

3. Sticking within your game's scope to meet original plans

With your penultimate chapter completed, it is now time to review everything we have covered within this book and how you can take your game design career forward. The final chapter will provide you with some parting tips and tricks and how to better yourself as you move beyond this book and take your next steps into this growing world.

CHAPTER 11

The End. Or Your Beginning?

This is it; you have completed all chapters within this book and have reached the epilogue of your journey. While we have considered some of the most important aspects within game design, we have also considered what you should avoid to best maximize your tIme, potentially money, and the skills you will learn or develop upon. But what have we covered so far?

- The history of video games and where they came from

- Took a deep dive into the industry job roles and the skills required

- 2D and 3D Unity tutorials

- Core elements of any game (mechanics, combat, and multiplayer)

- Creating your worlds and levels

- Designing of enemies and obstacles

- What makes a good HUD and how to make it effective for all players

And most importantly

- What is a game?

If you have followed this book carefully, you should hopefully have designed a great game idea and now ready to begin making it. But what happens once you have made it or in the process of making it? You will need to find a publisher who will publish your game. Of course, you can become a publisher and do it yourself, but this will be trickier if you have not got the funds or the exposure to your intended audiences. This means that you are going to need a pitch. Of course, we have created the Game Design Document and the other supporting documents, but you will need to create a pitch that you can use for a publisher.

© Michael Killick 2022
M. Killick, *The Way We Play*, https://doi.org/10.1007/978-1-4842-8789-7_11

A pitch is a streamlined presentation that shows the core parts of your game and is digestible for those listening. You will need to avoid showing the full contents of the story and any backstory of side characters, for example, and focus on the most important bits. But a pitch should be short and straight to the point. Too long and the audience will get bored, too short and the audience might be left confused and unsure on what the game is.

Microsoft PowerPoint or similar is perfect for creating the pitch. If you have used presentation software before, then you need to remember the basics of creating slides and delivering your pitch:

- Use a clear and simple font. You would be surprised on how many use fancy fonts that are not legible.

- Do not use too many slides for your pitch. If you have five minutes to sell your game, avoid using 20–30 slides. Keep it simple and straight to the point!

- A common mistake people make is to read information off the slide. This is one of the biggest mistakes to make in a presentation. If someone can read the information on your slide, then you should not be reading it to the audience! They can read it themselves! If you are going to have any writing on your slides, make sure they are bullet points that your audience can read so they know what you will be talking about, and then you explain each of them in detail. They are also a fantastic way for you to keep track of what you are talking about.

- Be clear in the way you talk. Any mumbling and your audience will struggle to hear you. This also goes for posture and presentation. Try to avoid slouching and always face your audience when you are talking. No one wants to be looking at your back when you are addressing them!

- Body language is key. Being open with your body will show you are friendly and willing to learn more from your audience as well as take any advice or constructive criticism.

While I am trying not to make this an idiot's guide to presentations, you would be surprised at how many people who forget the basics, and their presentation becomes muddled and hard to understand. I have sat through countless game pitches where the designers have been facing the screen and reading their slides instead of facing their panel to discuss their game idea. If you have lots to cover, then why not think about printing some notes that you can read from during the presentation? If this is a method you choose, make sure that you do not always look down to read the notes, keep looking up and make eye contact with the audience. You need to keep them engaged as much as possible!

Here is one bit of key advice I would like to share before we enter the pitch section. I have been part of many panels of game pitches, and in the middle of explaining the mechanics and designs of the levels, they say: "the player goes around the map." Do not say this! Saying "goes around" makes you look unprofessional and not clear on what your idea is. If you are going to say something like this, add some interesting adjectives instead such as, "Explore" or "Investigate". This will make your pitch clearer and flow better through your words. For example: "Nathan Drake traverses lost cities and uncharted territories to uncover lost treasure." "Batman leaves no stone unturned during his fight against the criminal underworld of Gotham City." Be creative when it comes to talking about the gameplay experience the player will have. If you can grip your pitch audience, then you can grip it to your target audience!

When thinking about creating a pitch, here are a few ideas on what you could have as titles for your slides. What detail you put into them will vary on your idea:

- Title and genre

- Synopsis of the story (make sure that this is a synopsis and not a novelization!)

- Mechanics and playstyle

- Intended audience and age rating

- Any moodboards or inspiration for your game (the better the image you can create in your audience's head about your game, the better!)

- Competitors within your chosen genre

- Any concept art

- Why your game will be successful and be above all others

Something else that would be perfect to show is a vertical slice of your game. A vertical slice is a demo version of your game. This should be the most polished version of your game with all the bells and whistles. This should be a level that characterizes what the game will look like in its entirety. If there is something playable, it will always swing in your favor! Sometimes, creating a demo is not possible, so do not strain yourself if you are trying to make one while preparing your pitch, but they will always be useful. If you have created a vertical slice, why not show some feedback you have gathered from a small audience? Bringing feedback to your pitch will help solidify opinions on your game and show that it has potential.

More than anything else, make sure that you are prepared. Practicing your pitch to friends or someone you know works within game design is the best way to ensure that you are ready for the big pitch. It is also worth getting feedback from your presentation so you can perfect your work and presentation method. Be excited about the game you are pitching. As we spoke about at the start of the book, the biggest fan of your game should be you! This also means that you need to be confident with the work you are presenting and knowing it inside out. If you do receive awkward questions either about the story or production plans, then you should feel confident with being able to answer them.

If you are working in a team and not fully confident with talking in front of people, ask someone else in the team to present for you, but make sure that you are still standing at the front so you can answer any questions you get. You also need to bring a backup of any work and the pitch with you. I have been on the panel for many pitches where game demos or the presentation failed to open. Always be prepared and bring an extra copy of everything!

If your pitch wasn't successful and the company or publishers would not like to take your idea further, then do not be disheartened by that. The key with pitches and game design is to keep trying. I have spoken and seen so many upcoming game designers who are too nervous to share their work in the worry that their ideas might be stolen or a mounting pressure that professionals from the industry will tear their ideas apart. This really is not the case! And the crucial thing that designers seem to forget when it comes to pitching to experts is that they are human. They will have been in your position at some point in their career, and they are at the point where they would like to share their ideas and wisdom to support new professionals. Designers will not make it anywhere unless they share their ideas. You never know who might be in the crowd or audience who loves your idea and gives you that boost you need. Selling yourself and your ideas is key to this vast gaming world. The way to make a name for yourself is by getting your name out there and sharing the work you create. Lots of professionals use platforms to develop and create their portfolio which is perfect for interviews and for personal progression. Here are a few platforms you might want to consider when making your portfolio:

- ArtStation

- DeviantArt

- Instagram

- LinkedIn

- Itch.io

- Creating your own website

All are remarkably simple and easy to set up. The more platforms people can find your name on, the wider reach you will have!

Another great way to start chatting to new people and work upon your game design skills is to sign up to some game Jams. These are game-making events where designers come together of all skill levels to create a game within a given time. With these, you can start to network with other like-minded designers and share knowledge and skills, as well as make games! It is also worth sitting in with any design talks from professionals in the industry. Attending game expos and taking part in some meet and greets is a great way to network while also getting some feedback on ideas but also advice about career progression within the industry.

Now with all your newfound knowledge, you have what it takes to begin designing your first game or taking an idea further. You are either about to start what I think is the best job in the world or continue your journey in this wide and exciting universe. There are some amazing and talented people within the industry who are willing to support you no matter the position you are in currently. The game industry is growing every day, so making friends in the right places will help you more than you know.

But before you begin to take your first steps, whether it be designing, looking for a job, or even starting out a new skill, the most important thing to remember is, no matter how big or ambitious an idea may be, show perseverance and keep going! There is no greater feeling than to know that you have overcome something and that you have achieved a goal. Always put your mind to something and never be afraid to show your creative flair and what it is you are capable of. Greatness will come from small beginnings!

APPENDIX

Game Design Document Template

The One-Sheet

This should be a simple document that contains the following details:

1. Game title

2. Intended game systems

3. Input methods and suggested save systems such as Cloud Gaming

4. Target age of players

5. Intended ESRB rating (Entertainment Software Rating Board)

6. Intended audience and supported languages

7. Summary of the game's story while also focusing on the gameplay

8. Clear modes of gameplay

9. USPs (unique selling points)

10. Any competitors

Make sure that all this information fits on one page!

The Ten-Page Boss

Page 1: Title Page

This should contain the following:

1. Game title

2. Intended game systems

3. Target age of players

4. Intended ESRB rating

5. Projected release date

6. Any plans for expansions for the game such as downloadable content (DLC) or extras that the player can purchase

Page 2: Game Outline

This should be split into the following two sections:

1. Game story

2. Game flow

Game story – An overview of the story without turning this into a novel. This should be a summary of the story so the readers can get a good idea on the trajectory of the game.

Game flow – This should be a summary of the game and the locations that game will be set. Keep this clear and cover areas such as the progression and rewards, gameplay, and challenges.

Page 3: Characters

Who is the main character going to be? How will they tie into the gameplay and what will their story be? What is their personality going to be like? Think about the important aspects of the main character and what the reader needs to know when reading this document. Will there also be any other playable characters in the game? How will these other characters differ from the main?

Page 4: Gameplay

What is the gameplay going to be like? What is the player going to do in the game? You need to provide as much detail as possible to explain the important aspects of your game. Think back to your USPs and how they will be incorporated here.

Page 5: Game World

This is where you talk about the world the game is set in and what it will look like. Think about the inspiration you have taken for the game and include as many visuals as you can. The better the image you can create for the reader, the better!

Page 6: Game Experience

What do you want your player to feel? What would be the point of the player playing a game without getting an experience? This could be about the camera, cinematics, or music. What will make your player experience full?

Page 7: Game Mechanics

This is where you explain fully about the mechanics of your game and how they will be incorporated into your levels. How will they help with the overall gameplay experience? Think about the USPs for the game and what you have stated earlier in your GDD. What will make your product stand out from others?

Page 8: Enemies

Enemies are a large feature of a game, and this is where you will need to explain how they will play a part in the story and the character. State their purpose and what they will do.

Page 9: Cutscenes

If your game will have them, cover them here and what the player will see in them. Also, state when they will appear in the game such as during a level, start, or end.

Page 10: Bonus Materials

For your final page, you will need to state any extra materials you want to feature in your game, such as New Game+, collectibles, and anything extra the player can do while trying to achieve 100% completion.

The GDD

Your final section should contain details of the following:

- Storyboards

- Diagrams

- Short animations

- Shareability

Beat Chart

Your final section covers progression and how the player begins the game and moves through the game. This should also focus on gameplay and how certain elements of the game are introduced.

Don't forget, if you need a recap about each of these sections, refer back to Chapter 1!

Index

© Michael Killick 2022
M. Killick, *The Way We Play*, https://doi.org/10.1007/978-1-4842-8789-7

H

I, J, K

Printed in the United States
by Baker & Taylor Publisher Services